PENGUIN PLAYS
PL69
TRAVERSE PLAYS

Traverse Plays

EDITED WITH AN INTRODUCTION
BY JIM HAYNES

PENGUIN BOOKS

Penguin Books Ltd, Harmondsworth, Middlesex, England
Penguin Books Pty Ltd, Ringwood, Victoria, Australia

—

A Wen and *Orange Soufflé* first published in *Esquire* magazine 1965.
Copyright © Saul Bellow, 1965.

La Manivelle first published 1962. Copyright © Robert Pinget, 1962.
Published in English as *The Old Tune* by John Calder 1962.
English adaptation copyright © Samuel Beckett, 1962.
La Musica first published by Gallimard 1965. Copyright © Marguerite Duras, 1965.
English translation published in Penguin Books 1966.
Translation copyright © Barbara Bray, 1966.
Translation from the Japanese of *The Lady Aoi* first published by Alfred A. Knopf Inc. 1957.
Published in Great Britain by Secker & Warburg 1957.
Copyright © Alfred A. Knopf Inc., 1957.
Allergy first published by Penguin Books Ltd 1966. Copyright © Cecil Taylor, 1966.
The Master of Two Servants first published by Penguin Books Ltd 1966.
Copyright © George Mully, 1966.
The Local Stigmatic first published by Penguin Books Ltd 1966.
Copyright © Heathcote Williams, 1966.

Made and printed in Great Britain
by C. Nicholls & Company Ltd
Set in Monotype Garamond

CONTENTS

INTRODUCTION

THE one-act play has indisputably been a major 'item' among the forces which have so radically changed the theatre in this century. A serious regard for the one-act by artists and public alike has made it possible for more new serious authors to have their work seen rather than read than could ever have been the case had the vogue for full-length evening works retained its hold. Indeed it has only been in the last ten or fifteen years that the one-act has emerged as a completely accepted form in the professional theatre world. One of the long-standing differences between amateurs and professionals was the formers' loyalty to the one-act form; but the plays that have changed the theatre radically in recent years have frequently been one-acts. This is not entirely because the importance of a new author is first revealed in early plays which are invariably one-acts; it is also because presenting a one-act play with a sense of standard and purpose catches the audience enough off guard for a genuine receptiveness to be achieved. One could cite endless examples of the effectiveness of the one-act play and still be no closer to the distinctive powers of the form itself; for the concept of *la pièce bien faite* is alien to the one-act and there are not, so far, any rules for writing one-act plays. In the one-act play, the author works innocently, self-indulgently, and gives loose rein to that lyric vanity which is (or could be) his style. The perfect example, I feel, is Ionesco, whose one-acts are architecturally enormous, and dwarf his full-length works.

Why should this be so? There are a number of passage-ways leading away from this question, the least explored probably being a little research into interval psychology. In an interval in a theatre where a full-length play is being performed the *entr'acte* intensity is a curious thing indeed. One can ask the question why are they there in the bar (ignoring, mercifully, the question of why they are there in the theatre)? They seek, usually in vain, to relieve their physical and maintain their mental restraint. They are busy assimilating or

7

appearing to have assimilated what they have seen, and sharing an excited anticipatory moment. Much of this can be said of any theatre evening, but with a full-length play the author is there in the bar with them. When a playwright feels himself obligated to what an audience expects from an evening in the theatre, too many of his thoughts are likely to turn from production to delivery. In short, in the never-ending war between the author and the audience a full-length play moves the play into the audience territory.

The author of a one-act, seldom aware of the plays with which his work will appear, will strive for unity and individuality at all costs, and the modesty of the form itself makes the evaluation a much simpler process. There is endless argument about quality in full-length plays, but a one-act play is a naked thing and even the best of productions don't have time in the space of a one-act to cover a basic flaw. From a producer's point of view the one-act play offers the variety of a season in a single evening. At the Traverse, where we go through sixteen or seventeen new productions a year, many of them bills of two or three one-act plays, variety is hardly a problem. We produce established authors for novelty. But in the average theatre repertoire a one-act play by an unknown author can be an enormous justifying thing in certain sensitive eyes. At heart every producer (I use the word producer in the American sense – i.e. management) wants to show new authors, but there are so many and the gamble is so great that it is normally neither possible nor wise. With a bill of three short plays he can put in a 'safe' name and still safely help new authors find an audience. Nothing is more satisfying for a producer than to discover an author and be the first to show his work. I don't really know why this should be so. Perhaps it is a way of showing the artistic community that producers are not really hostile, just cautious; and a way of encouraging the commercially minded that too much caution is bad business. At the Traverse it has been a trifle depressing to note that the sweet smell of the West End has instantly made some of our playwrights more aggressively commercial than we are ourselves.

For an actor, or an audience who are stimulated by acting,

an evening of several plays with the same cast in contrasting roles is enormously rewarding. The two Saul Bellow one-acts in this volume, as performed by Doreen Mantle and Harry Towb under the direction of Charles Marowitz, made a kaleidoscopic display of talent and temperament. Similarly the unexplained violence of 'The Local Stigmatic' was paired in its Traverse production against the mounting pressure of Pinter's 'The Dwarfs'.

But it is the playwright, surely, who has the most to gain and to learn from a one-act play. A theory or a philosophy may be put into a one-act and have an existence in a non-literary form without substance, development or conclusion being demanded. For it is more acceptable to put a big idea into a small play than the converse. (That is not to ignore the fact that what is wrong with most one-act plays is that they try to say too much, i.e. they try to be full-length plays.) A playwright can show his developing style or can conceive and create specifically in the form. The one-act play can be to the author either a phase or a form, with equal success. The Taylor play, 'Allergy', is the product of a rash of plays by Mr Taylor on the subject of socialism, seriousness and send-up; and is a perfect example of a work by a playwright and an idea in development. This in no way invalidates the play; it merely gives the play a somewhat more original look. The ideas it is concerned with are still new to the author as well as the audience, and a freshness results.

The Marguerite Duras play, 'La Musica', and the Robert Pinget play, 'The Old Tune', fall somewhere between these two delineations, as either may be taken as a short story in play form or as an embryonic segment from a longer play. 'The Lady Aoi' and 'The Master of Two Servants' (originally an opera libretto) are very much self-contained one-act plays. But the vital thing remains: that the author's work and thought is shown upon the stage as truly in a thirty-minute one-act as in a four-hour worrying over some three-act problem, and to me personally and to the Traverse as an organization (and we hope as a force) authors are our problem, our concern, our love, our business.

JIM HAYNES

SAUL BELLOW

A Wen

All inquiries concerning performing rights, professional or amateur, readings or any other use of this
material should be directed to the author's agent:
A. M. Heath Ltd, 35 Dover Street, London w1.

A Wen was first performed at the Traverse Theatre in May 1965, with the following cast:

SOLOMON ITHIMAR   Harry Towb
MARCELLA MENELIK   Doreen Mantle

Directed by CHARLES MAROWITZ

SCENE ONE

A dark stage. Upper left we see a regularly beating light. It descends and is revealed as the cage of an elevator. Inside is SOLOMON ITHIMAR, *Ph.D., a celebrated scientist, middle-aged. As the elevator door opens the stage lights up. We are in the lobby of a third-class Miami Beach resort hotel. A* LADY *is seated alone at a coffee table. She is of an age with* ITHIMAR *and has an ample, swelling figure, curving lips and a heavy head of kinky golden hair. Her name is* MARCELLA VANKUCHEN, *née* MENELIK. *The hour is sunset. Hurricane Clara has recently passed through. We now hear the first gusts of Hurricane Delia.*

ITHIMAR [*eagerly advances, then stops*]: You are. . .!

MARCELLA [*turning, she presses the many strands of beads to her bosom*]: Yes. . .?

ITHIMAR: Mrs Vankuchen? Marcella?

MARCELLA: You are the gentleman who rang my room and said he was a friend of my brother Julius?

ITHIMAR: I am Solomon Ithimar. [*He waits, keenly excited, for the name to take effect. He is disappointed.*]

ITHIMAR: From Detroit originally, now Washington, D.C.

MARCELLA: I was born in Detroit.

ITHIMAR: Of course. You and your brother Jemby, both.

MARCELLA: Jemby! His family name. No one has used it in more than thirty years.

ITHIMAR: You lived on Singleton Street, before it was paved. There were still horses.

MARCELLA: What was that name again?

ITHIMAR: Solomon Ithimar. That means nothing? [*Sighs, but is determined to continue.*] And you are Marcella Menelik!

MARCELLA: Was.

ITHIMAR: To me always will be. Your father was Marcus Menelik, the butcher. A red shop front with a golden bull's head.

MARCELLA: Brass.

13

ITHIMAR: Golden. Your mother's name was Faigl. She owned a player piano.

MARCELLA: Poor Mama – gone. Papa too.

ITHIMAR: Your dog's name was Gustave. He must have had a hernia. He groaned when he ran.

MARCELLA: It's all very far away, isn't it.

ITHIMAR: Your grandfather had a long beard. He had a newsstand. Your uncle Selig was a cigar-maker. Then there was your grandmother. She was called Basha. I have never forgotten any fact about your family. She wore a wig. I think she must have been a great beauty once. She had a dark, lovely, tender, even magical spot on her cheekbone. – It has meant a lot to me. Right here it was. [*Taps under his eye.*]

MARCELLA [*to herself*]: Ithimar? Ithimar? Must have been neighbours. [*Shrugs.*]

ITHIMAR: You had two maiden aunts, Dunya and Manya. Both nice. Dunya taught Russian. She was very *kulturny*. Manya was more *sympathisch*, however. [*He lowers his voice to accommodate a most significant feeling.*] She had the same little spot on her face as your granny, a speck of mulberry colour. Hers was on the upper lip, close to the nose. Or maybe she was a small bit cross-eyed. But terribly vivacious and charming. What a sharp little laugh! And the way she would rest her hand on her belt and draw a breath – such a bosomy breath! To watch her breathe made me feel like an astronaut. I believe we used to say an aeronaut, in those days. Anybody who went up in a plane or a balloon. Ah! [*Rubs his hands in sheer excitement. Moves his feet, sways somewhat.*]

MARCELLA: You do just like a chained elephant with your feet. First the right, and then the left, and then you knock them together. So you were a playmate of Jemby?

ITHIMAR: I was your playmate even more, Marcella.

MARCELLA: I didn't play with boys often.

ITHIMAR: Yes. Not often. But you played – you played.

MARCELLA [*a little impressed by the forcefulness of the assertion*]: Ithimar. . . . Was your father in the ice business?

ITHIMAR: No, he was the watchmaker on Windsor Street.

MARCELLA: Of all things! I remember him. He had one of

those clocks under the glass bell. And you've kept in touch with Julius all this time?

ITHIMAR: Not really close touch. No.

MARCELLA: He did a smart thing.

ITHIMAR: What was that?

MARCELLA: Giving up the shoe store, becoming a photographer.

ITHIMAR: Art for business?

MARCELLA: Art? Crap! Excuse me. But no Detroit wedding is a wedding unless it has an album by Menelik. We thought his diabetes would slow him up. Uh-uh! And have you noticed how photographers push people around? And that they all take it? Even the greatest in the land. And what do you do, Mr Ithimar? Are you married? Children? In business? I think they used to say the watchmaker's son was a prodigy.

ITHIMAR: An exaggeration.

MARCELLA: But you look well. That's no twenty-two-fifty jacket you're wearing. What's the label? Tailor-made. Three hundred dollars. Let me see that stitching. So, then, why are you staying in this dump? Let me see if I can figure you out. You've made a hobby of old times in Detroit. But you're not common. You must have done all right for yourself. [*Sips her drink.*] You don't boast. I'm from the small world, where everybody talks big. You must be from the big world, where you can afford to be modest. Just look how modest and conservative he is. My only criticism is that a man with such large feet shouldn't wear tapering trousers. I can't place you, except that your father fixed clocks. Oh, wait! You must be the scientist. Ye gods! You! A famous man. The clockmaker's son. You won the Nobel Prize!

ITHIMAR: Not I. My team.

MARCELLA [*shrieks*]: You're eminent! You made the atom bomb in Chicago.

ITHIMAR: I was in the Manhattan Project. [*He is unwilling to speak of this.*]

MARCELLA: Oh! [*Presses her painted nails to her brow.*] I could kick myself in the head! It's Iggy. Little Iggy. Iggy the

Genius. Einstein's protégé. Truman's scientific brain. The kid who put our neighbourhood on the map. How would I know what! I'm just a vulgar painted *yachna*, bad at canasta, so I could never understand high mathematics. [*Looks about.*] What are you doing in a joint like this? Though I'm glad to see you, and it's even kind of an honour, I have to ask myself, do angels smell of garlic? I mean, does a great scientist stay in a fourth-rate Miami dump, with bad sewage? And does he pick the hurricane season when nobody in his right mind comes?

ITHIMAR: I am on my way to an international conference. I thought I'd fly by way of Florida and take a very short holiday in the sunshine.

MARCELLA: What is this conference?

ITHIMAR: I can't say.

MARCELLA: Is it classified information?

ITHIMAR: Top secret.

MARCELLA [*guessing*]: You came to this loathsome place to avoid publicity – the press. [*She thinks.*] But then again. . . .

ITHIMAR: I knew you were here. [*The phone rings very loudly. He starts and exclaims:*] I won't take any calls!

MARCELLA: But you don't have to. Anyway, the clerk is out. This is the hour when the guy comes from the Syndicate and they do their bookie accounts in the men's room. You wouldn't know about such things. You take the big view. Overall. International. Cosmic. Nature.

ITHIMAR: Nature? I don't know Nature. I only know certain mathematical structures. Nature I don't understand. [*Silence.*]

MARCELLA: You're here alone. Of course. . . .

ITHIMAR: But I'm married. Children. That's what you want to know.

MARCELLA: I too. I have a son. Six foot four, two hundred ten pounds. Size sixteen shoes. Size twenty collar. How strange your breathing sounds. Is it something allergic? Or is the evening air too sweet for your nose? It's tropical evening, plus low tide, plus the septic tank. They're expecting Hurricane Delia.

ITHIMAR: You *are* marvellous! I was not wrong. I couldn't

have been wrong. I should have had more confidence in my instincts.

MARCELLA: And should you ask what am I doing here, the doctor sent me.

ITHIMAR: You aren't sick, are you, Marcella?

MARCELLA: The doctor is my husband. He's a mere chiropodist, but he gets very angry if you call him mister.

ITHIMAR: What is he like?

MARCELLA: Oh, he doesn't have a very piercing personality. He likes being typically American. He wears only white silk socks, which he buys by the gross. He smokes bad cigars. Is pompous about his chiropody. He's lazy – won't go down the hall; he pees in the sink. I don't hold it against him. It's all the usual good and bad. He acts cheerful but feels gloomy. Drives a Cadillac. And you have to call him Doc, or he blows up. It's an ordinary life. Boring. It'll kill us by and by. Maybe that's what we deserve. I don't know what it's all about.

ITHIMAR: Don't be sad. You're not dead, and life can always start again.

MARCELLA: Never the same, Iggy. You can't fool a woman with that sort of talk. Only men can deceive themselves that way. This is a swampy hotel. I stay here because my husband does all the feet for the management. But you . . .

ITHIMAR: The literature made it sound attractive.

MARCELLA: No, Iggy, you have another reason. Are you in trouble? Running away from the Pentagon? Mixed up in a spy plot?

ITHIMAR: Of course not.

MARCELLA: I can't believe it! You came here because of me. [*She stands.*] Me! [*She bursts out laughing.*] Me, me, me! [*She screams like a night bird.*] Dull old me!

ITHIMAR: That's right, Marcella. You.

MARCELLA: Me, with this face, with this figure! Are you out of your mind?

ITHIMAR: It's true I shouldn't be here, Marcella. It's wrong. Infantile. Illegal. Grotesque. Everybody will be sore. The thing is dangerous. It gives me a sick ache to think of it.

But here I am. Everything is green, indigo, swampy. Palms. Mangroves. The moon. I should have landed in Geneva, Switzerland, this morning. I was expected. This will be serious . . .

MARCELLA: Is it a government matter?

ITHIMAR: Multigovernmental. International. Disarmament. Top secret. Take my word for it. I can't say a word more.

MARCELLA: Instead, you flew to Detroit, looking for me, after thirty-five years. You saw Jemby. He told you where I was. . . . Because you were in love with me three dozen years ago?

ITHIMAR: I want you to listen to me. [*Strides to desk and looks behind it. Shuts a door. Tries to draw curtains, which blow out of his grasp.*] Something I haven't been able to get out of my mind.

MARCELLA: Iggy, I am a faithful wife. It's a fantastic and yet basically uninteresting fact nobody cares about. Still, the mind of a genius might discover what *is* interesting about me. According to certain ideas in the world there's nothing to me. Even I share those same ideas. They make me tiresome, more tiresome. But the intelligence of a man of distinction might see that after all . . . but I don't know after all what.

ITHIMAR: There *is* something extraordinary.

MARCELLA: Don't tell me here. I couldn't bear for other people to come in. I want it to be in private. [*Takes him by the hand.*] What's in your attaché case?

ITHIMAR: Documents, a slide rule. Things like that. My Rollax Razor. I never carry valises. [*They go towards elevator.*]

MARCELLA: Did you really know Einstein?

ITHIMAR: Yes. [*They enter elevator.*]

MARCELLA [*laughing as stage darkens and the elevator begins to rise*]: Oh, what a thing! What an occasion! All this way to see a childhood darling. And finding *me*! A square old creature. Only *you* remember.

[*The light throbs in the cage. A blast of wind is heard and simultaneously the current is cut off.*]

ITHIMAR [*after a long silence in the darkness*]: What is it?

MARCELLA: A power failure. [*Ithimar turns on a flashlight.*] Where did you get that?

ITHIMAR: The reading light is poor on the jets. I designed this, with a lens attached to magnify. [*He demonstrates on his own face. We see, about eight feet from the ground, a distorted mask of* ITHIMAR. *He turns the light on her and we see a similarly distorted mask of* MARCELLA.]

MARCELLA: Don't do that, Iggy. Please.

SCENE TWO

The light goes on. ITHIMAR *and* MARCELLA *enter* MARCELLA'*s room.*

ITHIMAR: May I pour myself a drink? [*He gulps from the bottle.*] Now, Marcella. [*She seats herself on large sofa, centre.*] For old times' sake, listen without prejudice. Just consider the peculiarities of another human being, the strange twists of his life. No reflection on you. I had to come here.

MARCELLA [*enjoying the word*]: Was it a compulsion?

ITHIMAR: Why else would I risk my security clearance, forget my official duties, to say nothing of the cause of international peace and who knows what else!

MARCELLA: Iggy, my husband banished me here, ostensibly to take off weight. But life surprises everyone. All I expected in Florida was ashes and gloom. So this is a gift from heaven. What unknown relationship have I enjoyed with you? Or do you want to drop it all, now that you see me in the flesh.

ITHIMAR: No, Marcella! Your colour has changed – a *little* – since those days. But then, both organisms have undergone such transformations as all human tissue must.

MARCELLA: Yes, your eyes seem to lean against your nose. They used to be more independent.

ITHIMAR: But as you will see, I have not ignored the years. But I'd better plunge straight in. What good is lecturing. Marcella, on your grandfather's back stairs in Detroit we played a game called 'Show', I believe.

MARCELLA: Called Show? Just you and me?

ITHIMAR: We showed each other things.

MARCELLA: What things! [ITHIMAR *sighs deeply, shakes his head.*] This is quite a thing to remember, four decades later in Florida before a storm. A reason to be absent from Geneva. Oh, Iggy! You, a Stockholm Laureate – me, a poor ordinary member of Hadassah. And *this* is our common ground . . . that you showed me your . . . that I showed you . . . that's what *you* say, anyway.

ITHIMAR: You did.

MARCELLA: I was not like that.

ITHIMAR: It's stamped into my memory – the green clumsy staircase. Noise from the house. Then the secret moment of intimacy which silenced the whole world. When you disclosed that personal object, you and I were sealed in stillness. Then my soul took form, a distinct form. I experienced all the richness and glory of existence for the first time consciously. I recognized beauty. And I loved it. With love came worship. I showed you what I had. It throbbed. It filled. It brought all being to a point, and that point could only aim towards you. . . .

MARCELLA: And that never happened again?

ITHIMAR: Repeatedly, but only approximately, and never so purely, with such perfection or clarity of vision. There have been moments, in certain discussions of Quantum Theory. With Niels Bohr, at times, I felt similar things. But that was sublimation. Not the thing itself.

MARCELLA: Quantum?

ITHIMAR: Listen to the rest, and listen with sympathy, please. I never forgot. It has been of tremendous influence in shaping my mind. And here is a strange aspect of that vision – that you have a little birthmark – a wen.

MARCELLA: Do I?

ITHIMAR: You're not aware of it?

MARCELLA: Absolutely not!

ITHIMAR: What your grandmother had on her cheek, and your Aunt Manya on her lip, that charming, colourful spot. My spirit has attached itself to it and gravitates about it.

To the scientist only a drop of pigment, perhaps, a small concentration of melanin, a purplish or rosy or mulberry discoloration; but to me a fixed star, an electromagnetic potency, a phenomenon which makes me ache, adore, throb, long to merge, and in fact seems to contain the secret of life.

MARCELLA: Oh! And where is it?

ITHIMAR: It *was* to the left as I faced ... [*stammers*] that little ... apricot-coloured; soft ... I didn't touch. I refrained. But a sense of softness entered my fingertips of itself.

MARCELLA: It even gives me an odd sensation now.

ITHIMAR: Don't you have a corresponding memory?

MARCELLA: You know how one-sided life is. We're all in business by ourselves.

ITHIMAR: May I have another drink?

MARCELLA: Help yourself. [ITHIMAR *swigs again from the bottle.*]

ITHIMAR: There have been times, as I was roller-skating to my laboratory, or talking to the President, when that little mark would suddenly appear to me. Sometimes like a closed bud or tinier. Sometimes the size of an egg. Or as if you held that egg to a powerful light, all transparency. Finally, the same diameter as the sun. The sun itself, where the fusion process goes on, pouring out subatomic particles. Lastly, explosions within me like whole novae, scattering my matter through sidereal space to cool again. Finally, I had to see you. I had to fly. I was driven. I had to know.

MARCELLA: To know what?

ITHIMAR: Whether I could still feel as I felt on that day.

MARCELLA: At your age?

ITHIMAR: I am not offended. That's also what I have said to myself. And yet, a vision is a vision. They say bliss is no miracle, only instinctual. I, however, do not believe in schematic approaches. My way is to test things out, not to decide beforehand on the basis of general experience. Who knows?

MARCELLA: I can't believe you would really ask me. ... [*She titters, then says sternly*:] Impossible! [*She gathers herself up.*] There are limits, Dr Ithimar. Because my husband is a mere chiropodist, don't think you can hold me cheap.

ITHIMAR: Don't talk yourself into a false attitude, Marcella. I think I understand how such a request must strike you. But how can you deny me! Think what I may recover. And if me, why not you?

MARCELLA: You're trying to work me up with illusions.

ITHIMAR: There are powerful forces at work, forces of all magnitudes. I mean my desire is *pure*. I am prepared to die without recovering that dimension of experience if it is irrevocable. But would you ask me to go to the grave resigned never to attempt the recovery?

MARCELLA: Why not resigned? What are you so special, Iggy? Are you too good for the common lot?

ITHIMAR: The matter isn't entirely personal.

MARCELLA: It might be different if you said, 'Marcella, I once loved you. And after all these years I love you still. Madly!' But it isn't me. It's just a wen or something. I don't remember it. I don't even know if I have it.

ITHIMAR: Why shouldn't you have it?

MARCELLA: Maybe it's all in your mind.

ITHIMAR: There's only one way to find out.

MARCELLA: It's not I personally who inspires you with this passion.

ITHIMAR: Who knows what will result.

MARCELLA: This is one of those menopause ideas that drive people to destruction. I'm not ready for that yet. And thank God I have a little dignity left yet. There isn't much I do have left. I'm reduced to bragging about my son's weight. Iggy, it's true, I'm very unhappy. I don't like to admit that unhappiness has broken me down to the point of absurdity.

ITHIMAR: But, Marcella, after all we mustn't expect to understand these deeper motives. The Prince was mad for Cinderella's foot. And think of King David and the virgin. How that poor kid must have felt when the old man applied her to himself. We have to tolerate these seemingly absurd things. Marcella, let me see.

MARCELLA: No. I'm sure it's changed. Everything has become different. There's a difference of forty years, nearly.

ITHIMAR: I beg you, Marcella. [*Carefully kneeling.*] I throw myself at your feet. [*Fastidiously, even pedantically, he extends himself before her.*] We are both unhappy. [*She tries to move away and he takes her foot.*] Marcella, don't refuse me.

MARCELLA: To tell the honest truth, Iggy. It's too grotesque for me.

ITHIMAR [*sits up, still holding her foot*]: Now you've said it.

MARCELLA: What have I said.

ITHIMAR: I've been trying to purge life of its grotesque elements. Ordinary life has a grotesque dimension, and this has become a theme of the times. The human mind is the slave of its own metaphors. When I sit at the White House in conference, I think of this. Individual fantasy collaborates with the grotesque inventions and achievements of the public realm. I see how people rejoice in their grotesqueness, and I see that reason must sever its dependency on the grotesque. We thrust the same distortion upon conscious events as we experience in dreams. The purpose of this distortion is to show that we must passively submit, as in dreams. So we remove all occasions of action and decision by making them grotesque. The grotesque is therefore our form of Quietism. It is the American form of Hindu Quietism.

MARCELLA: I don't follow that at all.

ITHIMAR: I was at Göttingen in 1931, studying Physics. One day I fell in the street and a fellow student tried to help me up. I yelled at him, 'Let me alone!'

MARCELLA: Why was that?

ITHIMAR: I had been thinking out a problem, and as I was falling a new mathematical expression entered my head. I didn't want to be disturbed. You see the occasion seemed grotesque, but it was redeemed by an ecstasy, by devotion to pure truth, by the ennoblement of reason.

MARCELLA: I still can't see where *I* come in.

ITHIMAR: Oh Marcella, let me see – let me see! [*He kisses the hem of her skirt.*]

MARCELLA [*to herself, bitterly*]: Well, nobody else cares about it at all. Just the gynaecologist, once a year or so. [*To* ITHIMAR:] Suppose we do look – big deal! And what then.

I don't want to exaggerate, but I do lose something. Respectfully means something to me. Not much. But it's better than absolutely nothing. I have to live, too. So I'll be making a sacrifice. And what will you sacrifice for me?

ITHIMAR: I'm in trouble already.

MARCELLA: You can claim amnesia. You may be able to get out of it easily. No, you must give up something of value, too.

ITHIMAR: Humble me.

MARCELLA: Don't carry on. I don't think you're very proud anyway. No, we'll put this thing on a real basis. You want me to give up my dignity? You must tell me. . . . Yes, you must tell me a classified secret. A top secret.

ITHIMAR: You want me to betray my country? Our country?

MARCELLA: Betray? Am I a Communist? Do I belong to any organization besides Hadassah and my Temple Sisterhood? No. I will swear to you never to tell, but you must give up one major secret. We don't know what goes on, the people of this country. What do they really do in Washington? The Invisible Government. The C.I.A. The Joint Chiefs. What about Flying Saucers. Are there really Flying Saucers?

ITHIMAR: Not that I know of.

MARCELLA: You aren't levelling with me. That wasn't truthful. What is this thing worth to you?

ITHIMAR: Ask me for any *personal* sacrifice. Ask me to inject something into my veins. To bail out with a parachute. To take a sailboat out in this hurricane. I'll do that.

MARCELLA: What do you tell President Johnson when you confer?

ITHIMAR: We talk about Atoms for Peace. We talk about detection devices, limited test bans, things like that.

MARCELLA: This I can read in the papers. You must tell me something I don't know.

ITHIMAR: All right. But. . .

MARCELLA: I'll make good. Right behind this sofa . . . to conceal you from any possible intrusion. Now tell me.

ITHIMAR: There is a device. Electronic. So minute it's invisible. Can be introduced anywhere. Works on the germanium diode principle. No bigger than a grain of pollen. It floats after the person one wants to watch. There are these invisible units which tell us, for instance, what Khrushchev is doing, any time of the day or night. Or Castro. Or Mao Tse-tung. The information is received in a special chamber of the Pentagon. On a screen.

MARCELLA: Great God! Is this true?

ITHIMAR: What would you like me to swear by?

MARCELLA: Who knows what those devils carry on. While they feed us nonsense. How many of these devices are there?

ITHIMAR: I don't know. I can go to prison for revealing this.

MARCELLA: No one will ever find it out from me.

ITHIMAR: Well? Now?

MARCELLA: Please don't be rough, Iggy. [*The hurricane is howling.*]

ITHIMAR: Why behind the sofa.

MARCELLA: You must make some concession to my feeling for propriety. Don't expect me to be brazen. With an extraordinary request like this. . . . Oh, the gullibility of women. The things we go along with! [*She leans against the sofa.* ITHIMAR *is now out of sight.*] You'd better remove my stockings. What are you doing with those buckles.

ITHIMAR: Perhaps you'd better remove your own girdle.

MARCELLA: Don't ask that. I can't. No, don't pull from the bottom. Here. From the top. You can't say I didn't humiliate myself. I hope you'll have the decency to keep all comments to yourself. [*She reaches under her dress to help.*] I never expected *ever* to find myself in such a situation.

ITHIMAR [*from below*]: Ah!

MARCELLA: Well? [*A pause.*] Not the way you remember, I'll bet.

ITHIMAR: I didn't expect it to be.

MARCELLA: You'll be happy to go back to your Quantum Theory.

ITHIMAR: There'll have to be a search.

MARCELLA: You don't intend to use that flashlight.

ITHIMAR: I'm terribly sorry.

MARCELLA: Your hands are shaking.

ITHIMAR: Well, it's pretty dense here, in places.

MARCELLA: I know you're going to be horribly disappointed and let down. If I had an illusion like yours, I wouldn't have taken such a risk.

ITHIMAR: May I ask you to bend just a little backward.

MARCELLA: Kindly be careful. I have a slipped disc. [*She bends further over back of sofa.*] You can be positive of one thing: I'll never give away any secret of yours, with what you're getting on me. Dr Ithimar, for heaven's sake, stop. What are you getting into. I won't permit any more. You must stop!

ITHIMAR [*gives a cry*]: It's here! [*His arms with flashlight flung up from behind sofa.*] I have it! Bless you, Marcella, you have it. You have it. You still have it!

MARCELLA: Where did you find it.

ITHIMAR: Here – here! Just where I remembered.

MARCELLA: I'll add it to my blessings on the next count. [*Hurricane noises. Clashing of fixtures.*]

ITHIMAR: With this point for a compass, I could make a new sweep of the universe.

MARCELLA: Is it having a result?

ITHIMAR: Marcella, it's happening again to me. Just as it did on those ancient stairs. I am beating – like a metronome. Beating.

MARCELLA: I will not look. That was not part of the bargain. [*Hurricane. The lights go out.*] I wonder if this old building will stand. Hurricane Clara slashed off the roof. Hurricane Delia may push the whole rotten place over. [*By flashlight, the two stare at each other.*]

ITHIMAR: This is a moment of awe. The dead years have shifted aside. Again I feel like that immature boy. You must look, too, Marcella. The results must be verified.

MARCELLA: I will not! [*But she does.*] Iggy, what are we going to do with it?

ITHIMAR: I don't know.

MARCELLA: Iggy, those invisible gadgets you told me about, no bigger than a grain of pollen, is one of them trained on you? Are you important enough?

ITHIMAR: At Los Alamos, I had two bodyguards. So perhaps I am.

MARCELLA [*in a shout*]: In a secret room at the Pentagon, is someone watching you and me on a screen.

ITHIMAR: Maybe. I've been in government service for so long, though. They must remember all I've done.

MARCELLA: But you're being seen. You're in danger.

ITHIMAR [*cries out*]: I don't care. I don't care. It's worth the price. We have recovered life. We were lost and now are found again. Found in a spout of blood as powerful as this hurricane!

MARCELLA [*piercingly*]: Iggy! What are you *doing*! This is grotesque. [*Great hurricane noise.*]

ITHIMAR: Let me alone. I have found the expression. I have it! [*Flashlight extinguished. There is a great roar as the curtain falls down, and afterwards the sound of cracking beams.*]

MARCELLA [*screaming*]: It's ending. We're falling. It's crashing. [*After silence, throatily:*] Oh, Iggy – This is the end!

CURTAIN

SAUL BELLOW

Orange Soufflé

All inquiries concerning performing rights, professional or amateur, readings or any other use of this
material should be directed to the author's agent:
A. M. Heath Ltd, 35 Dover St, London w1.

Orange Soufflé was first performed at the Traverse Theatre in May 1965, with the following cast:

PENNINGTON   Harry Towb
HILDA   Doreen Mantle

Directed by CHARLES MAROWITZ

Scene: HILDA's *apartment, a kitchenette-bedroom, in Indiana Harbor, Indiana. A counter or room divider separates the kitchen from the sleeping-quarters-cum-living-room. The furniture is old-fashioned; by contrast, what can be seen of the kitchen is quite modern. It is a wintry afternoon.* HILDA, *a middle-aged prostitute, is dressing old* PENNINGTON, *a very ancient millionaire. At curtain she has already gotten him into his long johns. She is treating him with special care; he is evidently puzzled by this unusual solicitude, and as he sits on the bed, tousled and feeble, he tries to penetrate her motive with his sharp, clear eyes.*

HILDA: Please sit straight, Mr Pennington. How can I button your chest if you slump. I know you get so relaxed, you droop.

PENNINGTON: Ha!

HILDA: Yes, relaxed. Up, chin, till I get the top button. That's it. I often wondered, Mr Pennington, do you import these garments?

PENNINGTON: Italian.

HILDA: You have them tailored overseas. A far cry from Montgomery Ward. [*Feels the collar with her finger first from the left, then the right.*] Silk trim. All your accessories are so elegant.

PENNINGTON: Talkative?

HILDA: Oh, why not? Why be so formal after all these years. Ten years.

PENNINGTON: Since my seventy-eighth birthday.

HILDA: Once a month. A hundred and twenty times. If I were one of your regular employees, I'd have plenty of seniority by now. [*Rising, she takes whisk broom and begins to brush his jacket.*]

PENNINGTON: Brushing?

HILDA: I've always been extra attentive. You just never noticed.

PENNINGTON: My powers of observation are famous throughout the financial world.

HILDA: Then maybe you've seen how good I've been for you. Why, the first time you had to be carried up the stairs.

PENNINGTON: Carried? Nonsense. Helped a little. My trick knee was acting up. I was the only man hurt in the Battle of Manila Bay. As I ran along the deck with a message for Admiral Dewey I fell on a winch.

HILDA: Poor Monty! [*She opens an ironing board and begins to iron his necktie.*]

PENNINGTON [*stiffly*]: Monty? Monty?

HILDA: What was the message?

PENNINGTON: You've never called me Monty.

HILDA: Well, Christ's sake, ain't it about time? You get very familiar with me.

PENNINGTON: That's another thing.

HILDA: The things you expect me to do – and say. The old-fashioned expressions you made me learn.

PENNINGTON [*fairly proud of himself*]: I get carried away.

HILDA: Such a woman in my position is supposed to hold back nothing, allow anything. Here, put your arm into this shirt.

PENNINGTON: You see what I mean? Usually you just pull it over my head.

HILDA: What? I never. You're mistaken. You always get the most classy treatment here.

PENNINGTON: Madame Hilda, during the first year you behaved like a member of the bomb squad with a suspicious parcel.

HILDA: That's not true.

PENNINGTON: Would I forget it? When I said, 'Undress me,' you bit your lip and had tears in your eyes.

HILDA: The pollen count is the real explanation.

PENNINGTON: And treated me like a mummy afterwards. You couldn't wrap me up fast enough. When I got home, my valet couldn't understand how I got so screwed up.

HILDA: It was only a matter of practice.

PENNINGTON: Perhaps my physique took some getting used

to. Honestly, did my big bones scare you? [*No answer.*] Pressing a tie with a hot iron makes the silk shiny. It'll smell peculiar, too. Hand it over. [*She gives it to him. He passes the tie nearsightedly before his eye.*]

HILDA [*sitting beside him and helping him into the shirt*]: The first time the chauffeur brought you in his arms and put you on this bed. It wasn't a weak knee, you were weak all over.

PENNINGTON [*joyously, almost hooting*]: Not all over! Not all over!

HILDA: If you're still going strong ten years later, it's no accident. Even you must admit it.

PENNINGTON [*looks about as she puts in his cuff links*]: You're like me. You don't want to change or move. It's a nice little place, for what it is. Except for the location.

HILDA: Surrounded by the steel mills, the coke ovens, the gas refineries, the brewery on the right and the soap factory behind. It's bright as day at midnight, and I hear the freights and cattle cars. And I never once even asked you . . . whether you're a major stockholder in any of these companies.

PENNINGTON [*surprised*]: What do you know about such things?

HILDA: Why shouldn't I? I read the papers, and that includes the society page, the financial section.

PENNINGTON: Aren't you peculiar today.

HILDA: I never asked you – you should've asked me.

PENNINGTON: What?

HILDA: Like, did I need advice. Like, do I have a problem. I got my problems, like anyone else. Taxes. Savings. You never gave me a tip on something. You know what I mean. I could always use a little capital gains, a little depreciation.

PENNINGTON: What about my socks?

HILDA: Don't get in an uproar. What's it any skin off your nose if I ask a plain question. I read up on politics, too. I wrote a letter to Congress about reapportionment. [*Starts towards copy of the letter.*] I kept a copy.

PENNINGTON [*angry*]: No! Don't pester me. I come here for certain things and not other things.

HILDA: But why keep everything in pigeonholes? Breakfast

in Libertyville. Business on La Salle Street. Golf one place, social life another place, and sex once every thirty days between three-thirty and five p.m. out in the dirty slums, between the lousy swamps and bulrushes and soap factories. You could swing a whole lot more.

PENNINGTON: That's just the way it happens to be. [*Pause.*] The first eight or nine years you didn't get personal at all.

HILDA [*taking his stiff leg on her lap and putting on one garter*]: No, you didn't encourage it.

PENNINGTON: And I don't encourage it now.

HILDA [*her nostrils flaring*]: No, you pay good dough. You even up the fee.

PENNINGTON: One hundred, in cash, and you don't have to report it.

HILDA: Neither do you. [*She buckles the second garter.*]

PENNINGTON: Aren't we running a little early this afternoon?

HILDA [*putting on his socks*]: It's the same as always.

PENNINGTON: No, it isn't. [*Betrays some agitation.*] You've got me all twisted around today, and I don't like it. I've never been a troublemaker. I never asked for anything unusual. Did I ever make one single peculiar request? [*She is silent.*] And I know what people are. Me, I only need a little assistance.... Don't rush things.

HILDA: I never can get your long underwear to lie flat under your stockings.

PENNINGTON: My mother had the same problem.

[*Hilda quickly wriggles on the second sock, her hair falling over her eyes, and hurries to the counter, on the kitchen side. There she opens a large French cookbook.*]

HILDA: Flour, salt, sugar, baking powder.

PENNINGTON: What are you doing?

HILDA: Shortening, eggs, orange rind.

PENNINGTON: You rushed me through it. You think I didn't notice.

HILDA: Measuring spoons, and cups. All laid out. [*Rubs her hands.*]

PENNINGTON: The timetable's off by as much as twenty minutes. Well, at least finish dressing me.

HILDA: I'm making something nice. You get your money's worth.

PENNINGTON: What are you pulling, Madame!

HILDA: It's time you got wise to the 'what's really what', sir. You take too much for granite – I don't take you for granite. To me, you're not just some wham-bam-thank-you-ma'am kind. I know who you are, so why shouldn't you know me, who I am, finally?

PENNINGTON: Oh, God!

HILDA: What, I'm just on the hook all month like a telephone? I'm a person. When you're coming, I dust, I clean up, I spray a nice flavour all around. I never pester you about how I put out for you. It just proves I'm a true, honest-to-God personality! [*Calms herself.*] I'm cooking you something.

PENNINGTON: Cooking! I'm freezing. Come here and put on my pants.

HILDA: Just hold your horses. The stove is heating. That's so pleasant on a winter day.

PENNINGTON: If it's for me, I don't want any. What do people cook in Indiana Harbor – pig's knuckles and kapusta? I can't digest cabbage.

HILDA: Something you might enjoy – very, very light. An orange soufflé.

PENNINGTON [*trying feebly to rise, his voice somewhat stifled*]: Soufflé! I won't eat it! I'll clench my teeth! Where is my chauffeur? He should be back. What time is it?

HILDA: Otto will be back at five p.m. as usual. I know what you must be thinking, what does an Indiana Harbor Polack whore know from soufflé? You think I spend my whole life in the sack with teamsters and rough trade? Well, try to adjust your mind to the reality situation. I have dozens and dozens of interests. I got a certificate from the Cordon Bloo school.

PENNINGTON: When were you in Paris?

HILDA: Paris? I ain't even been to Warsaw. But I'm learning how to be from Paris. The Cordon Bloo has a branch in Gary, Indiana. Only one thing now, where's the bottle of

Cointreau? Orange soufflé without Cointreau you can't make. This is real Paris Cointreau – costs $9.35. [*Pause.*] Where's that little dish.... [*Rattling sheets of wax paper.*] Where the Christ is it ... excuse me. Ah, here.

PENNINGTON: What do you know about kitchens, baking, eggs! It's winter. Hand me my pants. Soufflé!

HILDA: I go shopping like other women. You think they don't let whores in the supermarket? Or maybe they've got separate steel carts marked 'for whores only'? Go and look at all those broads in pale lipstick, smoking, and figure out who's the married woman. To make ends meet some of those little married chicks do a trick or two and the husband sits for the kids and knows all about it. If wives can hustle, whores can bake. [*Rapidly beats the eggs.*]

PENNINGTON [*wrapping his legs in the blanket*]: For ten years everything was smooth.

HILDA: Ten years, but only twelve days in each year.

PENNINGTON: I do the best I can.

HILDA: And the rest of the time?

PENNINGTON: I don't interfere with *you*.

HILDA [*making angry noises with the bowls*]: You don't bother yourself about me. If you got enough dough, you can make the world stand still. You can tie it up like a horse and it'll be waiting when you get back. You never took any personal interest in me.

PENNINGTON: Is that so bad? People want to be *seen*. Sometimes they're better off invisible. Anyhow, that's what I think. I'm old enough to be myself. In fact, too old to be anybody else.

HILDA: And rich enough so you don't have to be a hypocrite. – That is a nice thing about you. I appreciate your character.

PENNINGTON [*interested now*]: Do you?

HILDA: What's a whore good for if you can't be yourself with her either? What's the whole point of a whore? Her opinions don't worry you. She frees your mind. If you flunk, she doesn't get sore. She doesn't cripple you with a lot of stupid love.

PENNINGTON: Till today, you've been perfect. [*He seems*

moved.] You may not know it, but these visits mean a lot to me. Sometimes I count the days. So why spoil things?

HILDA: Why, because I bake you something nice? You don't want to expand a little? I want you to know I have a lot of sides to me. I can cook and bake and serve and keep up a conversation with anybody. Wait until you see what kind of china I've got and linen and silverware. To you a soufflé belongs in the Pump Room where the coloured wear a turban. Why shouldn't we know each other better?

PENNINGTON: I know you plenty.

HILDA: Because of sex? I ought to know best how important it is. I never bum-rap it. But.... [*She shakes her head, studies the oven thermometer.*]

PENNINGTON: What I was as a captain of industry, what I was on the stock market, what I've been in real estate, that's what I've been here. That's the best of me there is, the truest anyway. Not what I was with my wife and sons. With them I did what I had to do, not what I wanted. [*With a strange emotion*] Why do people have to pry! The secret truth is the best, and let it to hell alone!

HILDA: Let me check now. The rind, the Cointreau, the nutmeg, the stiffener.

PENNINGTON: Stiffener?

HILDA: In she goes. [*Puts dish in oven, sets timer.*] I'm really famous for my soufflé.

PENNINGTON [*too weak to sound tart*]: In the gas-tank set.

HILDA: Don't be upset. You look so ruffled. You've got your feathers up. Let's put on your pants. [*She brushes his trousers.*]

PENNINGTON: I liked it better when things were business-like. It's upsetting this way.

HILDA: Who knows, things might become even better.

PENNINGTON: Or I might lose something valuable by tampering. I know what works. As long as it works, let it be.

HILDA: Mr Pennington, what's my name? What's the address here?

PENNINGTON: Your name is Hilda.... [*He hesitates.*]

HILDA: Hilda what? Come on. If you can't pronounce it,

37

spell it. You can't. You don't know what street this is. You couldn't get here if Otto quit. Lots of people would try to find out who am I, Hilda Schzlepanowski, where do I come from, did I have a father or mother or a husband or a kid, and how did I ever get into this racket!

PENNINGTON: But not me.

HILDA: You should have asked once, anyway, even if you didn't listen to the answer. Do you think I'm just a poor tramp? Well, I want to tell you something. When I first moved in here, I couldn't pay the rent. And now this building belongs to me.

PENNINGTON [*struck by this*]: This is your own property?

HILDA: From the cellar to the tar paper. The mortgage is paid off, too.

PENNINGTON: Then why do you . . .?

HILDA: Financially, I've been independent since 1959. For six years you've been my only client.

PENNINGTON [*as she puts on his pants, he gives a cry from the soul, or its neighbourhood*]: Oh Lord, Lord, Lord! I've always wanted things so simple.

HILDA: What's so simple? To arrive on this street in a Rolls-Royce? What do you think I tell the neighbours?

PENNINGTON: You tell them I'm your fairy godfather?

HILDA: *They* don't think I'm a dumb Polack. I have a lot of refined friends. I go all over. At the Cordon Bloo I rubbed elbows with the best people on the South Shore, country-club people, politicians' wives. You think I hang around with scrubwomen?

PENNINGTON: I knew you were discreet.

HILDA: We had one conversation the first time. That was all I needed.

PENNINGTON: I knew you wouldn't blab. I thought if I died in your bed, naked, a heart attack. . . .

HILDA [*bringing up a little table and starting to set it for tea*]: Did you think I'd phone the gossip columns? I'd say, 'Mr Montgomery G. Pennington of Lake Shore Drive, Eagle River, and Palm Beach, President of the Tower Town Club, Chairman of the Board, and once a member of President Wilson's Cabinet ... just croaked in my bed – come take my picture.'

PENNINGTON: Stop, stop, I felt we should talk it over.

HILDA: I had to promise to dress you and call the chauffeur.

PENNINGTON: Yes. For some reason I wouldn't want him to see me naked. And I still say....

HILDA: The idea of scandal bothers you.

PENNINGTON: Scandal? Nonsense! I was thinking of my wife. She'd have given my body to a medical school. She'd let the students cut me up. She was insanely jealous.

HILDA: But she passed away first.

PENNINGTON: Yes. [*Brief silence.*] You read it in the papers?

HILDA: Four years ago. You miss her?

PENNINGTON [*hesitant*]: She's much missed by everybody.

HILDA: I'm sure the Garden Club misses her. The zoo. The museum.

PENNINGTON: Sure, they miss her. She gave them that great collection of South American lizards. Caught every one of them herself. Parachuted out of a plane over Patagonia with a survival kit. Didn't survive.

HILDA: Do you believe in an after-life?

PENNINGTON: I worry about it.... What's that I smell?

HILDA [*starting violently*]: My soufflé! Where's your watch? [*Finds his large old-fashioned gold watch which hangs on a thick chain. Darts to the timer.*] It's only halfway. [*Her heart is beating. She presses it with both hands.*]

PENNINGTON: Hilda, why did you give up all your clients except me? Am I ... am I so special? [*Leans towards her.*]

HILDA [*smiling to herself*]: You don't have to ask.

PENNINGTON [*taking her hand*]: Terrific, eh? I hoped it was like that. Everything about me is wearing out, except. With other men, *it* goes first, they say. Not me. But sometimes I worried that you didn't care about me, really.

HILDA: No!

PENNINGTON: I was like an Indian when I was young, up in Wisconsin – strong, husky, big, straight, tanned.

HILDA: Were you actually in the Battle of Manila?

PENNINGTON: I'm not a hundred per cent sure.

HILDA: But you were in the Navy?

PENNINGTON: It seems so, often. I've had so many lives. But I believe I can remember how it was as a young sailor in Hong Kong. And Admiral Dewey was a sportsman. He played golf. Ike wasn't the first. Then I think I can smell the battle – the explosives. Dewey steamed away from the Spanish fleet. He thought he had only fifteen rounds left. A miscount! I was sent with the message. There were forty-five. It started to be dawn, with one of those tropical flashes. But the deck was like a coal tunnel. It smelled like a mine. And suddenly, when I fell, the sun, like sparkling spumoni, chocolate, green, white, and orange, like flamingoes. [*Hilda, on the bed, has drowsed off during this reminiscence. He is annoyed.*] Nobody sleeps while I'm talking! [*He goes on.*] I never liked old age. And now I'm it. It's loathsome. Eyes coated, ears filled with old hair, big hollow knee bones, paunch and shanks, veins like bayous. [*Raises his chin.*]

HILDA: You don't realize how a woman looks at things. I've seen guys come and go, all kinds. I know what counts.

PENNINGTON: A strange thing. I was always virile. It showed in business, too.

HILDA: You break all the records.

PENNINGTON: You don't mean it!

HILDA: I mean, a man like you can do what he likes, write his own ticket.

PENNINGTON: You're clever, Hilda. I wouldn't have known it.

HILDA [*setting out dishes*]: Did you ever see more beautiful bone china? And look at the napkins. [PENNINGTON *looks nearsightedly.*] I put a lot of time into thinking to myself. . . .

PENNINGTON [*catching at watch*]: Otto should be here. [*Tries to rise.*]

HILDA [*forcing him back on bed*]: Hold still, I'll put on your necktie.

PENNINGTON: Just knot it. I'll pull it into place myself. I couldn't breathe when you did it last time. And I couldn't loosen it.

HILDA: There we are. [*Stands back to admire her work*.] Look, Mr Pennington ... why should we see each other only a dozen times a year?

PENNINGTON: I might be able to manage every two weeks. I heard of a fellow who gives injections.

HILDA: It's not what I have in mind.

PENNINGTON: All this ... egg-beating, brushing, silverware. [*Startled*] Marriage?

HILDA: No, what do you think I am, a lousy schemer?

PENNINGTON: I'm a little reassured. But some complicated idea is rotting your mind. I can tell.

HILDA: Why should I lie? There is something.

PENNINGTON [*exclaiming*]: I guessed! I guessed! I guessed!

HILDA: Wouldn't it be swell if we could richen our relationship?

PENNINGTON: Relationship?

HILDA: There's a side to me you haven't seen.

PENNINGTON: I haven't seen both sides of the moon, either, and it's all right with me. It's just more craters, I'm sure of it.

HILDA: When I say there is something, why do you think it's a scheme?

PENNINGTON: Listen, my dear, you read the papers, you say?

HILDA: Sure I do, and the magazines too.

PENNINGTON: Then you know about the Gemini capsule.

HILDA: Those two Russians going up together, you mean?

PENNINGTON: That doesn't count. Americans. Listen: When they reach outer space, they're going to open the hatch. Then one of them will sit in the doorway and let his feet hang. Then, if conditions are right, he'll float outside on a wire or something. He'll glide along with the ship. Oh, imagine! Hundreds of miles above the earth. Hundreds of degrees below zero. [*He strikes his chest with the back of his fist*.] That's what I've been through in my spirit. Floating on a tether through empty space, and each time making it back inside the capsule after my visit to death and nothing. So don't bug me.

HILDA: I never bugged you once in ten years, but now I'm in

a squeeze. I have this sister, she lives in a slum, in urban renewal.

PENNINGTON: What's that to me?

HILDA: Sometime back, a truck fell on her, a trailer truck skidded on greasy pavement, it jackknifed, she was at the bus stop and boom!

PENNINGTON: Killed?

HILDA: Pinned. The fire department worked hours to get her out. She got some money out of it. The lawyer took one third, the doctor, plenty, but there was still enough from the settlement so she could be comfortable the rest of her life. However.

PENNINGTON: I knew that was coming.

HILDA: Along comes her son – and says he wants to be a daughter. He wants to be a female out-and-out. He says, I want to have an operation in Denmark. And he takes the twenty thousand dollars she was going to retire on. You follow?

PENNINGTON: I wish I could say no.

HILDA: Now they're opening a dress shop together, in Indiana Harbor.

PENNINGTON: Outer space is better.

HILDA: They made me give them the shop in this building.

PENNINGTON: On the corner?

HILDA: The same. My sister and her former son. Now I appeal to you ... give me this chance for something normal.

PENNINGTON: What's normal?

HILDA: Not to be hemmed in by freaks. That's not for me. I want to get some class in my life.

PENNINGTON: No, no, leave me out of it. I've got a date at my club.

HILDA: After a little soufflé. You never even asked for a glass of water in this house.

PENNINGTON: Okay, Madame, to the point.

HILDA: Have a little coffee first.

PENNINGTON: I don't want any. Will you finally tell me what you're up to?

HILDA: You have that big place in Palm Beach.

PENNINGTON: What'd you know about it?

HILDA: I seen it.

PENNINGTON: In Florida?

HILDA: In the Sunday supplement.

PENNINGTON: What's it got to do with you?

HILDA: Don't jump now. I'm gonna make you a proposition and I really want you to consider it.

PENNINGTON: What proposition?

HILDA: I want to go down there. That's all I been able to think about. Please, Mr Pennington, don't just say 'no'.

PENNINGTON: What? What the hell do you want to do there?

HILDA: I'd be the lady of the house. Like – a hostess, a chatelaine. I'd ... I'd run it. I'd entertain for you. You think I couldn't do it? I could surprise you. I'm terrific with people. They love me. God, they do! They're happy to see me! Even ladies are happy to see me. Oh, Pennington, get me out of here. They're moving in next month and I'll be trapped – my sister and her daughter Archie.

PENNINGTON: I thought life had no more surprises.

HILDA: I'd run that place like a dream. Soufflé isn't all I can make. Duck with oranges. Bouillabaisse. Karsky Shashlik. Barcelona Paella with lobster claws and capers. Five kinds of mousse. Wine, I know all about. Flower arrangements. Your guests would be wild for me. Us American minorities are the spice of life. And to show I'm on the level I'll sign any kind of paper.

PENNINGTON: I have to go.

HILDA: You have to listen. I'll make over my property so it'll go to your estate when I kick off. I don't want to leave it to my niece.

PENNINGTON: For once a man works out a good thing. For once! At last! After years of trying. A good thing. Naturally, it has to be ruined. It's not only you I like – it's you plus the squalor.

HILDA: A thing has got to be just the way you want it. Couldn't it be even a little bit the way I want it? Give a guy a little chance, Pennington. Try me at Palm Beach. If I

43

don't work out, what do you lose? You can trust me. No pay, on approval – how's that?

PENNINGTON [*his indignation is so great that he finds the strength to rise and reach for his jacket*]: Take this table out of the way. Where's my coat? My stick! [*Finding his cane, he stands straighter.*] Nobody has forced me out of character – not in the last sixty years anyway.

HILDA: Wait, it's almost ready.

PENNINGTON: My overcoat's there. [*Walks slowly towards closet.*] What is this, February? I'll see you in March.

HILDA [*quickly goes to closet and takes out his fur-collared coat*]: Here, put it on and sit down. You've just got to sit down.

PENNINGTON: I don't want to sit. I want to go.

HILDA [*as timer buzzes*]: Sit. It's ready, it's ready. [*She drapes coat over him, runs to stove. He leans on cane, waiting. She bends out of sight as he peers over counter. Then she rises, wearing asbestos oven mitts. In the round baking dish is nothing resembling a soufflé.*]

PENNINGTON: Is that it?

HILDA: I can't understand what went wrong.

PENNINGTON: You couldn't get it up. [*After a short pause the rich tones of a Rolls-Royce horn are heard.*] Ah, there's Otto with the car. [*Sets homburg on his head with trembling hands, puts on gloves.*] About time, too. [*Leans on counter, the better to point at* HILDA *with his cane.*] Stick to what you know, Madame. [*Exit.*]

HILDA: Once they get you down, they never let you up. [*Striking the oven with the skillet.*] Never, never!

CURTAIN

ROBERT PINGET

The Old Tune

ENGLISH ADAPTATION BY
SAMUEL BECKETT

All inquiries concerning performing rights, professional or amateur, readings or any other use of this
material should be directed to Calder and Boyars
Ltd, 18 Brewer St, London W1.

The Old Tune was first performed in Great Britain at the Traverse Theatre in October 1964, with the following cast:

GORMAN   Leonard Maguire
CREAM   Declan Mulholland

Directed by MICHAEL GELIOT

*Background of street noises. In the foreground a barrel-organ playing
an old tune. Twenty seconds. The mechanism jams. Thumps on the box
to set it off again. No result.*

GORMAN [*old man's cracked voice, frequent pauses for breath even
in the middle of a word, speech indistinct for want of front teeth,
whistling sibilants*]: There we go, bust again. [*Sound of lid
raised. Scraping inside box.*] Cursed bloody music! [*Scraping.
Creaking of handle. Thumps on box. The mechanism starts off
again.*] Ah about time!

[*Tune resumes. 10 seconds. Sound of faltering steps approaching.*]
CREAM [*old man's cracked voice, stumbling speech, pauses in the
middle of sentences, whistling sibilants due to ill-fitting denture*]:
Well, if it isn't – [*the tune stops*] – Gorman my old friend
Gorman, do you recognize me Cream father of the judge,
Cream you remember Cream.
GORMAN: Mr Cream! Well, I'll be! Mr Cream! [*Pause.*] Sit
you down, sit you down, here, there. [*Pause.*] Great weather
for the time of day Mr Cream, eh.
CREAM: My old friend Gorman, it's a sight to see you again
after all these years, all these years.
GORMAN: Yes indeed, Mr Cream, yes indeed, that's the way
it is. [*Pause.*] And you, tell me.
CREAM: I was living with my daughter and she died, then I
came to live with the other.
GORMAN: Miss Miss what?
CREAM: Bertha. You know she got married, yes, Moody the
nurseryman, two children.
GORMAN: Grand match, Mr Cream, grand match, more
power to you. But tell me then the poor soul she was taken
then was she.
CREAM: Malignant, tried everything, lingered three years,
that's how it goes, the young pop off and the old hang
on.

47

GORMAN: Ah dear oh dear Mr Cream, dear oh dear.
[*Pause.*]

CREAM: And you your wife?

GORMAN: Still in it, still in it, but for how long.

CREAM: Poor Daisy yes.

GORMAN: Had she children?

CREAM: Three, three children, Johnny, the eldest, then Ronnie, then a baby girl, Queenie, my favourite, Queenie, a baby girl.

GORMAN: Darling name.

CREAM: She's so quick for her years you wouldn't believe it, do you know what she came out with to me the other day ah only the other day poor Daisy.

GORMAN: And your son-in-law?

CREAM: Eh?

GORMAN: Ah dear oh dear, Mr Cream, dear oh dear. [*Pause.*] Ah yes children that's the way it is. [*Roar of motor engine.*] They'd tear you to flitters with their flaming machines.

CREAM: Shocking crossing, sudden death.

GORMAN: As soon as look at you, tear you to flitters.

CREAM: Ah in our time Gorman this was the outskirts, you remember, peace and quiet.

GORMAN: Do I remember, fields it was, fields, bluebells, over there, on the bank, bluebells. When you think.... [*Suddenly complete silence. 10 seconds. The tune resumes, falters, stops. Silence. The street noises resume.*] Ah the horses, the carriages, and the barouches, ah the barouches, all that's the dim distant past, Mr Cream.

CREAM: And the broughams, remember the broughams, there was style for you, the broughams.
[*Pause.*]

GORMAN: The first car I remember well I saw it here, here, on the corner, a Pic-Pic she was.

CREAM: Not a Pic-Pic, Gorman, not a Pic-Pic, a Dee Dyan Button.

GORMAN: A Pic-Pic, a Pic-Pic, don't I remember well, just as I was coming out of Swan's the bookseller's beyond there on the corner, Swan's the bookseller's that was, just as I was coming out with a rise of fourpence ah there wasn't much money in it in those days.

CREAM: A Dee Dyan, a Dee Dyan.

GORMAN: You had to work for your living in those days, it wasn't at six you knocked off, nor at seven neither, eight it was, eight o'clock, yes by God. [*Pause.*] Where was I? [*Pause.*] Ah yes eight o'clock as I was coming out of Swan's there was the crowd gathered and the car wheeling round the bend.

CREAM: A Dee Dyan Gorman, a Dee Dyan, I can remember the man himself from Wougham he was the vintner what's this his name was.

GORMAN: Bush, Seymour Bush.

CREAM: Bush that's the man.

GORMAN: One way or t'other, Mr Cream, one way or t'other no matter it wasn't the likes of nowadays, their flaming machines they'd tear you to shreds.

CREAM: My dear Gorman do you know what it is I'm going to tell you, all this speed do you know what it is it has the whole place ruinated, no living with it any more, the whole place ruinated, even the weather. [*Roar of engine.*] Ah when you think of the springs in our time remember the springs we had, the heat there was in them, and the summers remember the summers would destroy you with the heat.

GORMAN: Do I remember, there was one year back there seems like yesterday must have been round ninety-five when we were still out at Cruddy, didn't we water the roof of the house every evening with the rubber jet to have a bit of cool in the night, yes summer ninety-five.

CREAM: That would surprise me Gorman, remember in those days the rubber hose was a great luxury a great luxury, wasn't till after the war the rubber hose.

GORMAN: You may be right.

CREAM: No may be about it, I tell you the first we ever had round here was in Drummond's place, old Da Drummond, that was after the war 1920 maybe, still very exorbitant it was at the time, don't you remember watering out of the can you must with that bit of a garden you had didn't you, wasn't it your father owned that patch out on the Marston Road.

GORMAN: The Sheen Road Mr Cream but true for you the watering you're right there, me and me hose how are you when we had no running water at the time or had we.

CREAM: The Sheen Road, that's the one out beyond Shackleton's sawpit.

GORMAN: We didn't get it in till 1925 now it comes back to me the wash-hand basin and jug.

[*Roar of engine.*]

CREAM: The Sheen Road you saw what they've done to that I was out on it yesterday with the son-in-law, you saw what they've done to our little gardens and the grand sloe hedges.

GORMAN: Yes all those gazebos springing up like thistles there's trash for you if you like, collapse if you look at them am I right.

CREAM: Collapse is the word, when you think of the good stone made the cathedrals nothing to come up to it.

GORMAN: And on top of all no foundations, no cellars, no nothing, how are you going to live without cellars I ask you, on piles if you don't mind, piles like in the lake age, there's progress for you.

CREAM: Ah Gorman you haven't changed a hair, just the same old wag he always was. Getting on for seventy-five is it?

GORMAN: Seventy-three, seventy-three, soon due for the knock.

CREAM: Now Gorman none of that, none of that, and me turning seventy-six, you're a young man Gorman.

GORMAN: Ah Mr Cream, always the great one for a crack.

CREAM: Here Gorman while we're at it have a fag, here. [*Pause.*] The daughter must have whipped them again, doesn't want me to be smoking, mind her own damn business. [*Pause.*] Ah I have them, here, have one.

GORMAN: I wouldn't leave you short.

CREAM: Short for God's sake, here, have one.

[*Pause.*]

GORMAN: They're packed so tight they won't come out.

CREAM: Take hold of the packet. [*Pause.*] Ah what ails me all bloody thumbs. Can you pick it up.

[*Pause.*]

GORMAN: Here we are. [*Pause.*] Ah yes a nice puff now and again but it's not what it was their gaspers now not worth a fiddler's, remember in the forces the shag remember the black shag that was tobacco for you.

CREAM: Ah the black shag my dear Gorman the black shag, fit for royalty the black shag fit for royalty. [*Pause.*] Have you a light on you.

GORMAN: Well then I haven't, the wife doesn't like me to be smoking.

[*Pause.*]

CREAM: Must have whipped my lighter too the bitch, my old tinder jizzer.

GORMAN: Well no matter I'll keep it and have a draw later on.

CREAM: The bitch sure as a gun she must have whipped it too that's going beyond the beyonds, beyond the beyonds, nothing you can call your own. [*Pause.*] Perhaps we might ask this gentleman. [*Footsteps approach.*] Beg your pardon Sir trouble you for a light.

[*Footsteps recede.*]

GORMAN: Ah the young nowadays Mr Cream very wrapped up they are the young nowadays, no thought for the old. When you think, when you think.... [*Suddenly complete silence. 10 seconds. The tune resumes, falters, stops. Silence. The street noises resume.*] Where were we? [*Pause.*] Ah yes the forces, you went in in 1900, 1900, 1902, am I right?

CREAM: 1903, 1903, and you 1906 was it?

GORMAN: 1906 yes at Chatham.

CREAM: The Gunners?

GORMAN: The Foot, the Foot.

CREAM: But the Foot wasn't Chatham don't you remember, there it was the Gunners, you must have been at Caterham, Caterham, the Foot.

GORMAN: Chatham I tell you, isn't it like yesterday, Morrison's pub on the corner.

CREAM: Harrison's, Harrison's Oak Lounge, do you think I don't know Chatham. I used to go there on holiday with Mrs Cream, I know Chatham backwards Gorman, inside and out, Harrison's Oak Lounge on the corner of what was the name of the street, on a rise it was, it'll come back to me, do you think I don't know Harrison's Oak Lounge there on the corner of dammit I'll forget my own name next and the square it'll come back to me.

GORMAN: Morrison or Harrison we were at Chatham.

CREAM: That would surprise me greatly, the Gunners were Chatham do you not remember that?

GORMAN: I was in the Foot, at Chatham, in the Foot.

CREAM: The Foot, that's right the Foot at Chatham.

GORMAN: That's what I'm telling you, Chatham the Foot.

CREAM: That would surprise me greatly, you must have it mucked up with the war, the mobilization.

GORMAN: The mobilization have a heart it's as clear in my mind as yesterday the mobilization, we were shifted straight away to Chesham, was it, no, Chester, that's the place, Chester, there was Morrison's pub on the corner and a chamber-maid, Mr Cream, a chamber-maid what was her name, Joan, Jean, Jane, the very start of the war when we still didn't believe it, Chester, ah those are happy memories.

CREAM: Happy memories, happy memories, I wouldn't go so far as that.

GORMAN: I mean the start up, the start up at Chatham, we still didn't believe it, and that chamber-maid what was her name it'll come back to me. [Pause.] And your son by the same token.

[Roar of engine.]

CREAM: Eh?

GORMAN: Your son the judge.

CREAM: He has rheumatism.

GORMAN: Ah rheumatism, rheumatism runs in the blood Mr Cream.

CREAM: What are you talking about, I never had rheumatism.

GORMAN: When I think of my poor old mother, only sixty

and couldn't move a muscle. [*Roar of engine.*] Rheumatism they never found the remedy for it yet, atom rockets is all they care about, I can thank my lucky stars touch wood. [*Pause.*] Your son yes he's in the papers the Carton affair, the way he managed that case he can be a proud man, the wife read it again in this morning's *Lark*.

CREAM: What do you mean the Barton affair.

GORMAN: The Carton affair Mr Cream, the sex fiend, on the Assizes.

CREAM: That's not him, he's not the Assizes my boy isn't, he's the County Courts, you mean Judge ... Judge ... what's this his name was in the Barton affair.

GORMAN: Ah I thought it was him.

CREAM: Certainly not I tell you, the County Courts my boy, not the Assizes, the County Courts.

GORMAN: Oh you know the Courts and the Assizes it was always all six of one to me.

CREAM: Ah but there's a big difference Mr Gorman, a power of difference, a civil case and a criminal one, quite another how d'you do, what would a civil case be doing in the *Lark* now I ask you.

GORMAN: All that machinery you know I never got the swing of it and now it's all six of one to me.

CREAM: Were you never in the Courts?

GORMAN: I was once all right when my niece got her divorce that was when was it now thirty years ago yes thirty years, I was greatly put about I can tell you the poor little thing divorced after two years of married life, my sister was never the same after it.

CREAM: Divorce is the curse of society you can take it from me, the curse of society, ask my boy if you don't believe me.

GORMAN: Ah there I'm with you the curse of society look at what it leads up to, when you think my niece had a little girl as good as never knew her father.

CREAM: Did she get alimony.

GORMAN: She was put out to board and wasted away to a shadow, that's a nice thing for you.

CREAM: Did the mother get alimony.

GORMAN: Divil the money. [*Pause.*] So that's your son ladling out the divorces.

CREAM: As a judge he must, as a father it goes to his heart.

GORMAN: Has he children.

CREAM: Well in a way he had one, little Herbert, lived to be four months then passed away, how long is it now, how long is it now.

GORMAN: Ah dear oh dear, Mr Cream, dear oh dear and did they never have another?

[*Roar of engine.*]

CREAM: Eh?

GORMAN: Other children.

CREAM: Didn't I tell you, I have my daughters' children, my two daughters. [*Pause.*] Talking of that your man there Barton the sex boyo isn't that nice carryings on for you showing himself off like that without a stitch on him to little children might just as well have been ours Gorman, our own little grandchildren.

[*Roar of engine.*]

GORMAN: Mrs Cream must be a proud woman too to be a grandmother.

CREAM: Mrs Cream is in her coffin these twenty years Mr Gorman.

GORMAN: Oh God forgive me what am I talking about, I'm getting you wouldn't know what I'd be talking about, that's right you were saying you were with Miss Daisy.

CREAM: With my daughter Bertha, Mr Gorman, my daughter Bertha, Mrs Rupert Moody.

GORMAN: Your daughter Bertha that's right so she married Moody, gallous garage they have there near the slaughter-house.

CREAM: Not him, his brother the nurseryman.

GORMAN: Grand match, more power to you, have they children?

[*Roar of engine.*]

CREAM: Eh?

GORMAN: Children.

CREAM: Two dotey little boys, little Johnny I mean Hubert and the other, the other.

GORMAN: But tell me your daughter poor soul she was taken then was she. [*Pause.*] That cigarette while we're at it might try this gentleman. [*Footsteps approach.*] Beg your pardon Sir trouble you for a light. [*Footsteps recede.*] Ah the young are very wrapped up Mr Cream.

CREAM: Little Hubert and the other, the other, what's this his name is. [*Pause.*] And Mrs Gorman.

GORMAN: Still in it.

CREAM: Ah you're the lucky jim Gorman, you're the lucky jim, Mrs Gorman by gad, fine figure of a woman Mrs Gorman, fine handsome woman.

GORMAN: Handsome, all right, but you know, age. We have our health thanks be to God touch wood. [*Pause.*] You know what it is Mr Cream, that'd be the way to pop off chatting away like this of a sunny morning.

CREAM: None of that now Gorman, who's talking of popping off with the health you have as strong as an ox and a comfortable wife, ah I'd give ten years of mine to have her back do you hear me, living with strangers isn't the same.

GORMAN: Miss Bertha's so sweet and good you're on the pig's back for God's sake, on the pig's back.

CREAM: It's not the same you can take it from me, can't call your soul your own, look at the cigarettes, the lighter.

GORMAN: Miss Bertha so sweet and good.

CREAM: Sweet and good, all right, but dammit if she doesn't take me for a doddering old drivelling dotard. [*Pause.*] What did I do with those cigarettes?

GORMAN: And tell me your poor dear daughter-in-law what am I saying your daughter-in-law.

CREAM: My daughter-in-law, my daughter-in-law, what about my daughter-in-law.

GORMAN: She had private means, it was said she had private means.

CREAM: Private means ah they were the queer private means, all swallied up in the war every ha'penny do you hear me, all in the bank the private means not as much land as you'd tether a goat. [*Pause.*] Land Gorman there's no security like land but that woman you might as well have been talking to the bedpost, a mule she was that woman was.

GORMAN: Ah well it's only human nature, you can't always pierce into the future.

CREAM: Now now Gorman don't be telling me, land wouldn't you live all your life off a bit of land damn it now wouldn't you any fool knows that unless they take the fantasy to go and build on the moon the way they say, ah that's all fantasy Gorman you can take it from me all fantasy and delusion, they'll smart for it one of these days by God they will.

GORMAN: You don't believe in the moon what they're experimenting at.

CREAM: My dear Gorman the moon is the moon and cheese is cheese what do they take us for, didn't it always exist the moon wasn't it always there as large as life and what did it ever mean only fantasy and delusion Gorman, fantasy and delusion. [*Pause.*] Or is it our forefathers were a lot of old bags maybe now is that on the cards I ask you, Bacon, Wellington, Washington, for them the moon was always in their opinion damn it I ask you you'd think to hear them talk no one ever bothered his arse with the moon before, make a cat swallow his whiskers they think they've discovered the moon as if as if. [*Pause.*] What was I driving at?

[*Roar of engine.*]

GORMAN: So you're against progress are you.

CREAM: Progress, progress, progress is all very fine and grand, there's such a thing I grant you, but it's scientific, progress, scientific, the moon's not progress, lunacy, lunacy.

GORMAN: Ah there I'm with you progress is scientific and the moon, the moon, that's the way it is.

CREAM: The wisdom of the ancients that's the trouble they don't give a rap or a snap for it any more, and the world going to rack and ruin, wouldn't it be better now to go back to the old maxims and not be gallivanting off killing one another in China over the moon, ah when I think of my poor father.

GORMAN: Your father that reminds me I knew your father well. [*Roar of engine.*] There was a man for you old Mr Cream, what he had to say he lashed out with it straight from the shoulder and no humming and hawing, now it comes back to me one one year there on the town council my father told me must have been wait now till I see ninety-five, ninety-five or six, a short while before he resigned, ninety-five that's it the year of the great frost.

CREAM: Ah I beg your pardon, the great frost was ninety-three I'd just turned ten, ninety-three Gorman the great frost.

[*Roar of engine.*]

GORMAN: My father used to tell the story how Mr Cream went hell for leather for the mayor who was he in those days, must have been Overend yes Overend.

CREAM: Ah there you're mistaken my dear Gorman, my father went on the council with Overend in ninety-seven, January ninety-seven.

GORMAN: That may be, that may be, but it must have been ninety-five or six just the same seeing how my father went off in ninety-six, April ninety-six, there was a set against him and he had to give in his resignation.

CREAM: Well then your father was off when it happened, all I know is mine went on with Overend in ninety-seven the year Marrable was burnt out.

GORMAN: Ah Marrable it wasn't five hundred yards from the door five hundred yards Mr Cream, I can still hear my poor mother saying to us ah poor dear Maria she was saying to me again only last night, January ninety-six that's right.

CREAM: Ninety-seven I tell you, ninety-seven, the year my father was voted on.

GORMAN: That may be but just the same the clout he gave Overend that's right now I have it.

CREAM: The clout was Oscar Bliss the butcher in Pollox Street.

GORMAN: The butcher in Pollox Street, there's a memory from the dim distant past for you, didn't he have a daughter do you remember.

CREAM: Helen, Helen Bliss, pretty girl, she'd be my age, eighty-three saw the light of day.

GORMAN: And Rosie Plumpton bonny Rosie staring up at the lid these thirty years she must be now and Molly Berry and Eva what was her name Eva Hart that's right Eva Hart didn't she marry a Crumplin.

CREAM: Her brother, her brother Alfred married Gertie Crumplin great one for the lads she was you remember, Gertie great one for the lads.

GORMAN: Do I remember, Gertie Crumplin great bit of skirt by God, hee hee hee great bit of skirt.

CREAM: You old dog you!

[Roar of engine.]

GORMAN: And Nelly Crowther there's one came to a nasty end.

CREAM: Simon's daughter that's right, the parents were greatly to blame you can take it from me.

GORMAN: They reared her well then just the same bled themselves white for her so they did, poor Mary used to tell us all we were very close in those days lived on the same landing you know, poor Mary yes she used to say what a drain it was having the child boarding out at Saint Theresa's can you imagine, very classy, daughters of the gentry Mr Cream, even taught French they were the young ladies.

CREAM: Isn't that what I'm telling you, reared her like a princess of the blood they did, French now I ask you, French.

GORMAN: Would you blame them Mr Cream, the best of parents, you can't deny it, education.

CREAM: French, French, isn't that what I'm saying.

[Roar of engine.]

GORMAN: They denied themselves everything, take the bits out of their mouths they would for their Nelly.

CREAM: Don't be telling me they had her on a string all the same the said young lady, remember that Holy Week 1912 was it or 13.

[Roar of engine.]

GORMAN: Eh?

CREAM: When you think of Simon the man he was don't be telling me that. [*Pause.*] Holy Week 1913 now it all comes back to me is that like as if they had her on a string what she did then.

GORMAN: Peace to her ashes Mr Cream.

CREAM: Principles, Gorman, principles without principles I ask you. [*Roar of engine.*] Wasn't there an army man in it.

GORMAN: Eh?

CREAM: Wasn't there an army man in it.

GORMAN: In the car?

CREAM: Eh?

GORMAN: An army man in the car?

CREAM: In the Crowther blow-up.
    [*Roar of engine.*]

GORMAN: You mean the Lootnant St John Fitzball.

CREAM: St John Fitzball that's the man, wasn't he mixed up in it?

GORMAN: They were keeping company all right. [*Pause.*] He died in fourteen. Wounds.

CREAM: And his aunt Miss Hester.

GORMAN: Dead then these how many years is it now how many.

CREAM: She was a great old one, a little on the high and mighty side perhaps you might say.

GORMAN: Take fire like gunpowder but a heart of gold if you only knew. [*Roar of engine.*] Her niece has a chip of the old block wouldn't you say.

CREAM: Her niece? No recollection.

GORMAN: No recollection, Miss Victoria, come on now, she was to have married an American and she's in the Turrets yet.

CREAM: I thought they'd sold.

GORMAN: Sell the Turrets is it they'll never sell, the family seat three centuries and maybe more, three centuries Mr Cream.

CREAM: You might be their historiographer Gorman to hear you talk, what you don't know about those people.

GORMAN: Histryographer no Mr Cream I wouldn't go so far

as that but Miss Victoria right enough I know her through and through we stop and have a gas like when her aunt was still in it, ah yes nothing hoity-toity about Miss Victoria you can take my word she has a great chip of the old block.

CREAM: Hadn't she a brother.

GORMAN: The Lootant yes died, in fourteen. Wounds.
[*Deafening roar of engine.*]

CREAM: The bloody cars such a thing as a quiet chat I ask you. [*Pause.*] Well I'll be slipping along I'm holding you back from your work.

GORMAN: Slipping along what would you want slipping along and we only after meeting for once in a blue moon.

CREAM: Well then just a minute and smoke a quick one. [*Pause.*] What did I do with those cigarettes? [*Pause.*] You fire ahead don't mind me.

GORMAN: When you think, when you think. . . .
[*Suddenly complete silence. Ten seconds. Resume and submerge tune a moment. Street noises and tune together crescendo. Tune finally rises above them triumphant.*]

CURTAIN

MARGUERITE DURAS

La Musica

TRANSLATED BY BARBARA BRAY

All inquiries concerning performing rights, professional or amateur, readings or any other use
of this material should be directed to the author's
agent: Margaret Ramsay Ltd, 14a Goodwin's
Court, St Martin's Lane, London wc2.

La Musica was first performed in Great Britain at the Traverse Theatre in May 1966, with the following cast:

MICHEL NOLLET   John Thaw
ANNE-MARIE ROCHE   Mary Yeomans

Directed by MILO SPERBER

*The entrance hall of a hotel. Street noises. To the left, two notices:
'Reception', 'Dining Room'. A clear space inside the entrance, but
to the right, reaching past the centre of the stage, the hall is arranged
as a conventional hotel lounge, with settee and armchairs, desk, and a
television set placed so that people watching it can be seen while the
screen remains invisible.*

*We hear certain members of the hotel staff but never see them: no
point in cluttering up the stage with the antique presence of waiters
and manageresses.*

*The two main characters are quite ordinary in appearance; there is
nothing about them to attract special attention.*

*The staging should be cinematic with the faces strongly lit for the
equivalent of close-ups and occasionally plunged in darkness. The rest
of the stage should grow gradually darker as the dialogue progresses.*

MICHEL NOLLET *enters left and crosses to the reception desk
[which is out of sight. We hear the following conversation off.]*

HE: Excuse me. Are you sure the nine-sixteen is still the only
train for Paris?

OLD LADY: I'm afraid so, Monsieur Nollet. Next year they're
going to start an air service three times a week, but in the
meanwhile ... Here's your key.

HE: I'm not going up, thanks. Could you get me a call to
Paris? The number is Littré 89-26.

OLD LADY: Littré 89-26. Certainly, Monsieur Nollet. Shall I
put it through to you in the Lounge?

HE [*hesitating*]: ... Yes, if you will, please.

[*He comes back into the lounge and stands by the desk waiting.*]

OLD LADY: This is the Hotel de France, Evreux. Could I have
Paris, Littré 89-26, please, and could you tell me how long it
will take? [*Pause.*] How long? [*Calling to Michel Nollet.*] It'll
be through in five minutes, Monsieur Nollet.

63

[*Longish pause. Then* ANNE-MARIE ROCHE *enters. She too crosses to reception.* MICHEL NOLLET *reacts when he sees her, but does his best not to show it. She doesn't see him.*]

OLD LADY: There's a telegram for you, Madame ... [*embarrassed*] Madame Nollet.

SHE [*quite calmly*]: Ah yes? I was expecting it.

[MICHEL NOLLET, *as well as the audience, is listening to the conversation.*]

OLD LADY: Here's your key, madame.

SHE: Thank you, I'm not going up. I just dropped in for the telegram ... I thought I'd go for a walk.

OLD LADY: You'll be surprised how much the place has changed. You can hardly recognize it round the station.

SHE: What about out at ... out at La Boissière?

OLD LADY [*embarrassed*]: La B——? Oh, I believe that's still much the same. ... But of course I don't go out much and I hardly ever get as far as that. ...

SHE: Well, I shan't be long.

OLD LADY: Very well, madame.

[*Pause.* ANNE-MARIE *comes back into the lounge, putting the telegram into her bag. She sees* MICHEL NOLLET *and stops. He looks at her and bows slightly. She just perceptibly nods in acknowledgement.*]

HE: I just wanted to say ... if there was anything you wanted me to do ... [*strained smile*] ... like the furniture that's in store ... I could arrange for it to be sent if you like, to save you the trouble.

SHE: Furniture? [*Then she remembers.*] Oh yes. No, thank you. [*Pause.*] I don't know yet what I shall be doing ... whether I want to keep it or not ... But thank you. [*Pause.*] Good night.

HE: Good night.

[*She goes out. Left alone, he lights a cigarette, still standing. He is agitated, but has himself almost completely under control. The telephone rings.*]

OLD LADY: Hallo? Is that Littré 89–26? Your call, Monsieur Nollet.

[*We hear the voice at the other end of the line, muted but quite clearly audible.*]

WOMAN'S VOICE: Is that you, Michel?

HE: Yes ... How are you?

WOMAN'S VOICE: I'm all right. [*Pause.*] Is it all over?

HE: Yes.

WOMAN'S VOICE: When?

HE: This afternoon.

WOMAN'S VOICE: I ... I hope it wasn't too ... painful.

HE: Well ... No, it was all right.

[*Silence. He can't make conversation.*]

WOMAN'S VOICE: Did ... did you see her?

HE: Of course.

WOMAN'S VOICE: ... And?

HE: Nothing. [*Pause.*] What do you want me to say? [*Slightly mocking.*] That's life, as they say ... Getting a divorce ... It's bound to be ... [*Pause.*]

WOMAN'S VOICE: What?

HE [*ironical*]: Well, let's say it's never easy.

WOMAN'S VOICE: Has ... has she changed?

HE [*It's a question he hasn't asked himself*]: Yes ... I suppose so. Yes. [*Pause.*]

WOMAN'S VOICE: Michel. Do you love me?

HE [*without hesitation, sincerely, but automatically*]: Yes, I do. [*Pause.*] Tomorrow then at three-seventeen at the Gare Saint-Lazare?

WOMAN'S VOICE: Yes, I'll wait at the main exit, that's the safest. [*Pause.*] We could go to the cinema in the evening if you like ...

HE: If you like.

[*Pause.*]

WOMAN'S VOICE [*with a sort of uneasiness, impatience*]: Will you tell me about it one day?

[*Pause.*]

HE: I don't think so ... But ... who knows? One day, perhaps.

WOMAN'S VOICE: But why?

[*He doesn't answer.*]

WOMAN'S VOICE: Forgive me.

HE: It's nothing ... [*To change the subject.*] What are you doing this evening, sweetheart?

WOMAN'S VOICE: Nothing, I've been in bed all day. [*Pause.*] Where is she staying?

HE [*hesitates, restrains himself*]: I don't know.

WOMAN'S VOICE: Have you had dinner?

HE: No. I thought I'd ring you before I went. This is the back of beyond. Everyone's in bed by nine.

WOMAN'S VOICE: Will you take me there one day?

HE [*A little laugh*]: Yes, why not? [*Pause.*] Well, see you to-morrow, sweetheart. Good night.

WOMAN'S VOICE: Good night, Michel.

[*He goes out. The entrance hall remains empty. A light is turned out. A clock is heard theatrically striking ten.*

ANNE-MARIE ROCHE comes in, smoking a cigarette. She wanders round the lounge, sees the television set, switches on and sits down to watch. We hear the end of the news.

MICHEL NOLLET comes in. She doesn't hear. He stands and looks at her; remembering something; with intense emotion. He looks at her: she is free again. He hesitates and finally goes and sits down behind her. She senses somebody there and turns round. The following dialogue goes very slowly.]

SHE: Oh! ... it's you.

HE [*getting up*]: Why shouldn't we talk to each other?

SHE: Why should we?

HE: No particular reason ... because we haven't got anything else to do.

[*She gives a grimace of distaste, bitterness, sadness.*]

SHE: Nothing could be more over and done with than ... than that.

HE [*hesitates, then*]: We could be dead ... Or were you including death?

[*He smiles. She doesn't.*]

SHE: I don't know ... But perhaps, yes ... perhaps including death.

[*He doesn't pursue it. She didn't want to speak in the first place, but goes on now to try to get rid of this constraint.*]

SHE: Thanks for offering about the furniture. I've thought about it ... I don't want it ... it'll just be in the way ... But if you'd like it ... [*Pause.*] We don't have to stick to the [*slight laugh*] legal division.

HE [*slight laugh*]: No, no thanks ... [*Thinking about something else.*] No, I don't want anything ... [*Pause.*]

SHE: What shall we do with it then?

HE [*still thinking of something else*]: I don't know. Nothing. Just leave it there.

SHE [*smiling*]: Right.
[*Silence.*]

HE: Would you like a drink?
[*She gestures 'why not'. He walks over towards reception and looks, without going off. Comes back.*]

HE [*smiling*]: Sorry, I think they've all gone to bed.

SHE [*smiling*]: It doesn't matter ...
[*She gets up. They don't quite know where to go from here. The banality of the following dialogue is exaggerated.*]*

HE [*trying to keep it light*]: The place is completely changed – have you seen?

SHE: It hasn't changed much out at La Boissière.

HE: No ... it's more towards the north, the development out towards where they're building the new aerodrome. You heard about that?

SHE: Yes, it'll be a great improvement – change everything.

HE: Did you go out there ... to La Boissière?

SHE [*looking at him in surprise*]: Yes, of course. I've never been back here since ... [*She smiles.*] You've just come back from there, haven't you?

HE [*surprised and confused*]: How did you know?

SHE: I thought I saw you at the top of the hill when I got there ... But I wasn't sure ...

HE [*looking away*]: Yes, I went past the house. [*Embarrassed pause.*] I didn't think the couple that bought it from us were so young as that, did you?

SHE: No ... it must have changed hands again since ... I

*Author's note: This passage can be extended, cut or modified.

didn't recognize the two people who were having dinner there tonight . . .

HE [*smiling*]: Yes . . . it was strange . . . the dining-room was arranged just as . . . just as it used to be. Even the television . . .

SHE [*continuing*]: And they weren't saying anything to each other . . . not a word . . . yes, strange . . .
   [*Slight laugh. Silence.*]

HE: They've finished the block of flats I started. Do you remember? Out beyond the race-course? . . .

SHE: I don't think I . . . Oh yes, I remember! Have they made a good job of it?

HE: Yes . . . it looks as though they kept to the plans.
   [*What can they say? He makes another effort.*]

HE: I suppose I ought to have come back now and again to make sure they were getting on all right . . . But I didn't . . . anyway, it's not too bad.

SHE: Is your work still going well?

HE: Not too badly, thanks. I've had a couple of very good commissions lately.

SHE: Are you still as mad about it as ever? [*She smiles. She must have been jealous of his work in the past.*]

HE [*smiling too*]: Yes, as mad as ever.

SHE: Good.

HE: Thanks. [*Pause.*] I suppose you're catching the nine-sixteen in the morning?

SHE [*hesitating*]: No. Someone's fetching me.
   [*Silence.*]

HE: It's funny . . . I don't even know where you live . . . someone asked me how you were the other day and I couldn't tell him.

SHE: Oh, I'm not really living anywhere for the moment . . . All over the place . . . mostly in the north . . .

HE: The north!

SHE: Yes . . . that's how it turned out . . . I quite like it.

HE [*with a smile that's already warm*]: You still hate the south as much as ever?

SHE: Yes, as much as ever.

[*Silence. They move to different places and the conversation changes direction.*]

HE: I haven't heard anything about you for two years.

SHE: Valerie gives me news about you every so often ...

HE [*starting slightly*]: Do you still see her?

SHE: Yes ... I ... I think quite differently about her now. You ... without being exactly prejudiced, it's not that, you can get into the habit of adopting someone else's views ... you ... without realizing it you're under their influence ... [*Pause.*] I see the Tourniers sometimes too. [*Pause.*] That's all, I think.

    [*These allusions, which are never repeated or explained, are to their common past.*]

HE [*risking it*]: I didn't think you'd come alone. I thought there'd be someone with you.

SHE [*with a shrug*]: No ... [*Pause.*] You came alone too....

HE: Yes ... I didn't think it was worth ...

SHE: No ...

    [*She indicates that she didn't think it was worth it either. They both smile very faintly. They look at each other properly for the first time. Enormous feeling of constraint; but curiosity is even stronger.*]

HE: ... Do you really mean, including death?

    [*The dialogue goes very slowly here. She doesn't answer.*]

HE: You said that nothing was more over and done with than ... than that. Even death.

SHE: I said I didn't know.

HE [*laughing*]: You know when you came back from Paris ... I was waiting for you at the platform....

    [*She looks at him. He looks down, stops laughing, doesn't go on. She gets up from her chair and walks about the room. He is not surprised that she cannot keep still. While she is still standing he presses it even farther.*]

HE [*sudden but polite*]: Are you going to get married again?

SHE [*equally abrupt*]: What happened on the platform?

    [*Silence. He hesitates, says nothing. She doesn't press it. Something resembling the old violence has just passed between them.*]

SHE: I'm getting married again in August.

HE: Three months ...

SHE: Yes, the legal interval ... It's stupid, but what can you do?

HE: Yes.

SHE [*letting him have it, but still not in an unseemly way*]: We shall be going away afterwards. Going to live in America. [*Pause.*] I want ... peace and quiet ... a bit late I know, even for that ... I've got to be quick, to make up for lost time ... [*Polite smile.*]

HE: So you think, now, that time doesn't always have to be lost?

SHE: Just a manner of speaking ... I've never thought about it ... Really, never. [*She restrains a laugh.*] And what are you going to do?

HE: Much the same as you, except that I have to stay in France because of my work.

SHE: Will you get married again?

HE: I don't know yet.
   [*He takes her in completely, from head to foot. She doesn't see.*]

HE [*almost involuntarily*]: You haven't changed.

SHE [*turns round quite suddenly; we see her face*]: I've aged, I know ...

HE: I didn't mean ...
   [*They are stirred.*]

HE: Yes, you have changed a bit in the face.

SHE: How?

HE: I think it's the eyes chiefly ... you used to have a very ... gentle way of looking at people ... and then as soon as they looked at you they could guess, more or less, what you were going to say.

SHE [*stiffly*]: That must have been very boring. [*She pretends to laugh.*]

HE: At the end, yes. During the last few months, very boring indeed.

SHE [*goes over and switches on the television. Nothing happens, the programme has closed down. She looks at her watch*]: Eleven o'clock already.
   [*Perhaps he hasn't heard.*]

HE: It's amazing, you and I standing here talking like this . . . [*He indicates himself and her with his hand.*] Do you remember those last months?

[*At last, they both burst out laughing.*]

SHE: Hell.

HE: Yes. Hell.

[*She shuts her eyes and tries with a wave of the hand to efface the image of what she sees. They gradually stop laughing.*]

SHE: I shouldn't think it could be as bad as that more than once in a lifetime, should you?

HE: What?

SHE: That Hell.

HE: I shouldn't think so [*pause*], or else . . .

[*We feel something stir between them again, but this time neither tries to get free of it.*]

HE: Or else experience, that beastly experience we hear so much about, is absolutely useless. . . .

SHE: No . . . you're wrong, I think . . . it's not that . . . If it happens again . . . I've thought about it since . . . if it happens again it must be because one hasn't discovered any other way of . . . [*She tries to find the words.*]

HE [*finding them*]: . . . of escaping from . . . fatigue, perhaps?

SHE [*eyes lowered*]: Yes, I think that's it. [*Pause.*] Don't you?

HE: Perhaps.

[*Silence. Memories crowd upon them more and more vividly.*]

SHE [*trying to remember*]: How long was it we stayed here in the hotel before we moved into the house? I can't remember how long it was before it was ready – three months? Six?

HE [*trying to remember*]: About three, I think . . .

[*It was here in the Hotel de France that the rarest part of their life together took place. They fall quite silent.*]

SHE: Isn't it strange we should find it so hard to remember?

HE: Some . . . moments come back more clearly than others . . . But I think what lies behind them counts just as much . . . you can't always tell.

SHE [*quite directly, but as if she were speaking about memory in general and not theirs in particular*]: And there are some moments that are absolutely clear.

HE [*the same*]: Hell, for example?

SHE: Perhaps ...

HE: Good times after bad?... reconciliations ... isn't that what you mean?

SHE: Yes. [*She seems to be trying to disperse the growing feeling between them by talking.*] If the story of every couple were governed by its own particular laws ... and I believe it is ... if every ... couple has its own fundamental way of ... and I believe it has ... then we ought never have moved into the house ... never have ... settled down ... we ought to have stayed on here in the hotel.

HE [*continuing her thought*]: And lived just like that ... going from one hotel to another ... like people in hiding?... like ...

SHE: Perhaps ...
[*Silence. Muffled explosion: what he was going to say was 'Like lovers'.*]

SHE: Don't you think...?

HE: Yes ... but then there was no reason why we should behave differently from everyone else. We were young, everyone approved of our getting married ... Everyone was happy, your family, my family, everyone ... We had everything we needed [*he laughs*], house, furniture ... your fur coat ...

SHE: We behaved just like everyone else. Yes.

HE: But we *were* just like everyone else, so there was no reason why we shouldn't have done ... what's usual ... the same as them.

SHE: And so we've finished up at the same point.

HE: Is that a question?

SHE: Perhaps ...
[*Pause.*]

HE: Yes, I think we have finished up at the same point as the others. Sometimes there's a divorce, sometimes not ... but perhaps ... perhaps the difference is negligible.

SHE: If it hadn't been now it would have been later ...
[*He doesn't answer.*]

SHE: Don't you think?

HE: What?

SHE: The ... end ... Don't you think?

HE: How can you say when ... you haven't tried ...

SHE: Yes, you can have an idea. Besides, what does it matter whether something lasts a long time or a short time ... if it's got to end anyway ... that's what one has to tell oneself ...

HE: In that case [*smiling*] everything is working out according to the rules.

SHE: Yes, of course. That too ...
    [*They are silent.*]

SHE [*very low*]: How stupid ...

HE: What?

SHE [*correcting herself*]: No. It's true – it's ... automatic ...

HE: ... You're starting all over again ... I'm starting all over again ...

SHE [*reacts involuntarily*]: Yes, but ...

HE [*continuing her sentence*]: ... this time we know that the end is inevitable?
    [*She doesn't answer.*]

HE: No?

SHE: Yes ... and no. We know that a certain kind of end is inevitable.

HE [*with difficulty*]: A certain kind?

SHE: Yes. The only kind ... but we also know there's no need to shout it from the rooftops ... we know you can dispense with [*slight laugh*] the third act.

HE: We were extremely young.

SHE: And now we don't want all that trouble, all that worry, we ...

HE [*interrupting*]: We've got other things to do?

SHE: I suppose so.

HE: What?

SHE [*laughing*]: Nothing. But I expect we've got a different way of doing it. [*Pause.*] We used not to shrink from anything ... at the drop of a hat there'd be sleepless nights, scenes, tragedies ...
    [*They laugh.*]

HE: Violence.

SHE [*hesitates and then confesses*]: And even worse ... [*The allusion is to an attempt at suicide.*]

    [*He is dumbfounded. He gets up and comes over to her. The second act of* La Musica: *she almost died, and he discovers it.*]

HE: What?

SHE: Yes. [*She laughs.*] Oh, yes.

HE: When?

SHE [*looking at him*]: When you asked for a divorce. But it wasn't really serious ... after all, here I still am ... it must have been just a vulgar attempt at blackmail.

    [*Clock theatrically strikes midnight. He is rooted to the spot by what he has just heard.*]

HE [*just a murmur*]: I had no idea ...

SHE [*low*]: How could you have? It was inconsistent, I know, but I asked them not to say anything to you.

HE [*involuntarily*]: But ... it's terrible! ...

SHE [*smiling*]: No, it's nothing ... the idiotic sort of thing everyone does. [*Pause. He says nothing.*] I shouldn't have told you ...

HE: No ... no ... I'm sorry.

SHE [*tries to change the subject, and at the same time to find out about him*]: Valerie's spoken to me about ... her ... She's ... very young, isn't she?

HE: Yes.

SHE [*absently*]: You don't know him ... you've never met.

HE: And ...

SHE [*understanding he means does she love the other man*]: Yes. Everything is all right. Everything is as it should be.

    [*They fall silent again. It is growing late. The memories crowd upon them ...*]

SHE [*slowly, painfully*]: We must go up. They're waiting to turn out the lights. [*She points towards reception.*]

HE [*roughly*]: Let them wait.

    [*Long silence.*]

SHE: No point in talking like that. We must go up.

HE [*using her name for the first time*]: Anne-Marie ... it's the last time in our lives.

[*She doesn't answer, but remains seated. They are silent a full minute. Then with a sharp but not unprepared transition, she begins to speak.*]

SHE [*there is an element of challenge in her voice*]: He was another man, not you. That was the main thing – he was another. On one side there was just you, and on the other there were all the men that I should never know. [*Pause.*] I think you must understand me quite clearly. [*Pause.*] Don't you?

HE: Yes.

SHE: I was sure you would. [*Pause.*] I think that at the moment ... we were quits.

HE [*crisply*]: Yes, we were that ... [*Pause.*] It's funny to hear the truth two years afterwards.

SHE: Interesting.

HE: I never knew ... what happened that time you went to Paris. What you told me ... then ... I don't suppose that was the truth.

SHE: You wouldn't have been able to bear the truth. Now, at this distance, you think you could have. But you couldn't.

HE: I couldn't bear anything. [*Attempt at a laugh.*]

SHE: Hardly anything. [*Pause.*] Nothing.
    [*Pause.*]

HE [*with difficulty*]: How did ... did it happen?

SHE: Oh, do we have to talk about it?

HE: No reason why we shouldn't indulge in the truth now.

SHE [*after an effort to remember*]: I met him standing up on a bus. [*Pause. She is almost reciting.*] Afterwards he waited outside my hotel. I saw him there once, twice ... the third time I was frightened, it was late, he was outside the hotel still, it was almost one o'clock in the morning and ... there you are.

HE [*roughly*]: Where had you been?

SHE: A night-club in Saint-Germain-des-Prés. [*Pause.*] You didn't know about that either, did you?

HE: No.

SHE: I used to go dancing sometimes ... you didn't dance ... I missed it, I think I must have missed it a good deal.

HE: It would have been all the same if I had danced.

SHE: Probably. [*A silence.*] You know, it's quite terrible the first time you're unfaithful ... awful. [*She laughs.*] It's true ... the first time ... even if it's only ... quite casual ... it's awful. It's quite wrong to say it's unimportant.

[*He is silent, smiling vaguely.*]

SHE [*going on*]: I don't think that for a man being unfaithful is ever so ... serious ...

HE: Was it because of him you put off coming back?

SHE: Yes.

HE [*painfully*]: Did you want it to happen or did it happen in spite of you?

SHE: I wanted it. I was desperate. I did it to try to recapture the first moments ... the first time. That was all like you, I did it to recapture those moments ... that can never be replaced ... [*Pause.*] But you know, the taste for that sort of adventure ... you get it from someone else.

HE: I'm glad you wanted it to happen ... I don't care about the rest. [*Slowly, with difficulty.*] And did you recapture the first moments?

SHE: One always does ... even ... at the worst ... even only for an hour ... you know that as well as I do ... that was why I did not want to come back. No other reason.

[*Silence. He is trying to look back beyond what happened in Paris.*]

HE: One afternoon, a few months before you went to Paris, I ... I saw you ... you didn't see me ... you were going along the street there [*he points outside*] and I followed you ... It was in the afternoon. I'd left the office to go and look at one of the building sites, and I saw you going into a cinema ...

SHE [*laughing*]: Oh, yes!

HE [*laughing too*]: I followed you in. They were showing a western that we'd already seen together ... You were alone ... near the front ... no one came and sat with you ... That evening you didn't say anything about it ... and I didn't ask any questions ... It was spring, three years ago ... you were sad sometimes already ... The next day, after lunch, I asked if you were going out. You said no, but you did. I followed you again. You went to the races ... still alone. I'd never dreamed ... [*Pause.*] I started to suffer. [*A silence. She remembers.*]

SHE: Yes, I used to do things like that.

HE [*with a smile*]: And do you still?

SHE [*laughing*]: Yes.

HE: I had you followed every day for a week.

SHE: And you didn't find anybody.

HE: No. Not that that made any difference. [*Pause.*]

HE [*resuming*]: It was terrible. I was jealous of you yourself ... of that secret part of you ... One day I followed you by car. You looked marvellous, there alone in your car. You were driving very fast ... You drove out about twenty kilometres and pulled up by a wood. You went into the wood and I lost sight of you. I hesitated and almost came after you, and then ... I just drove away. That's one of the absolutely clear memories that we were talking about just now.

SHE: But it's nothing, nothing at all, it's just my way of passing the time. [*Pause.*] I'd forgotten that drive. [*Pause.*] But you ought to have come and found me ...

HE: I was afraid of being in the way ... I thought you wanted to be on your own.

SHE: Yes, I did, sometimes.

HE: Don't defend yourself.

SHE: I'm not.

HE: There's no need ... I was still a bit intrigued by it, that's all.

SHE [*almost as she might have said it 'before'*]: You are funny. Why shouldn't one do things like that?

HE: No reason at all. But why say nothing about them?

SHE: There's no point.

HE: That's not true.

SHE [*bluntly, in the present*]: I've never seen the use of talking about things like that, and yet strangely enough ...

HE [*insisting*]: You could say, in the evening: I went to the cinema this afternoon.

SHE [*thinks for a moment*]: No. You see, you don't do that sort of thing at ... at the beginning ... so when you do start to do them it's better not to talk about it ... it would be misunderstood, wouldn't it ...

HE: Misunderstood?

SHE: Oh, some people spend the afternoon when love starts to languish ... I go to the races.

[*The light sinks lower. The clock theatrically strikes two. The room is almost in darkness. They don't move.*]

SHE [*very low*]: Two o'clock. What will people think?

[*He doesn't answer. The return of desire. He gets up as if he has made up his mind to leave it at that, and goes slowly over towards reception. She remains seated.*]

HE [*turning round*]: What number is your key?

SHE: Twenty-eight.

[*She gets up too. He comes back and they stand facing each other. He holds out her key. They do not move, she doesn't take it. He speaks very softly, assuming an unreal tone.*]

HE [*very gently*]: This is very silly, you'll be exhausted to-morrow. [*Pause.*] What time are you being called for?

SHE: I don't know exactly – some time before nine.

HE: Good-bye.

SHE: Good-bye.

[*She takes the key and they start to go off in opposite directions. But after a few steps they both stand still. He comes back, she is leaning against a chair, watching him. They are face to face.*]

SHE [*harshly*]: What happened on the platform?

HE: I wanted to kill you. I'd bought a gun and I was going to kill you as you got off the train.

SHE: In such cases the murderer is usually acquitted. Did you know that?

HE: I knew.

[*Silence. Anger. Despair. They stand stiff and motionless.*]

SHE: Why didn't you do it?

HE: I don't remember.

SHE: That's not true.

HE: It is. I've forgotten.

SHE [*insistent*]: Try to remember. You disappeared from the house that night without saying anything.

HE: Just a minute ... Ah yes, I drove to Cabourg. When I got there I threw the revolver in the sea. I thought that was what one did with a revolver ... [*He laughs.*] I'd read it somewhere.

SHE [*grim*]: Had you read about violence too?

HE: About that too.

SHE [*confesses*]: And I'd read about committing adultery in Paris.
[*Silence.*]

SHE [*exaggerated tone of aggressiveness*]: Well, what are we going to do about the furniture?

HE: Nothing.

SHE: That's absurd.

HE: Yes ... I don't know ...
[*It's clear that they are thinking about something else.*]

HE: Did you want it to happen or did it happen by chance?

SHE [*taken aback at first*]: You asked me that before.
[*He doesn't answer.*]

SHE [*finally*]: I didn't want it to happen.

HE: And was it true about your being desperate?

SHE: The novelty drove out the despair.
[*Pause.*]

HE: One Sunday afternoon, you weren't there, I don't remember now where you'd gone ... I went for a walk through the town and I met a girl, a foreign girl just passing through ... We went to a hotel. [*Pause.*] It was marvellous. I didn't love her, I never saw her again. It was marvellous. Simple.

SHE: Was it necessary?

HE: No, why? It was marvellous but it wasn't necessary. I loved you.
[*She moves away from him.*]

SHE: Have you any more questions to ask me?
[*Suddenly the sleeping hotel is filled with the sound of a telephone ringing. They do not move. Noise of someone moving about in reception, then the voice of the old lady.*]

OLD LADY: Hallo! Who did you want to speak to? [*Pause.*] Monsieur Nollet? Yes, he's in. [*Pause.*] Hold the line, please. [*Pause. Calling softly to* MICHEL NOLLET.] Are you there, Monsieur Nollet?

[*She knows they are both there.*]

OLD LADY [*calling, a bit flustered*]: Monsieur Nollet ...

HE [*hesitates*]: Yes, I'm here.

[*He goes over to the telephone, trying to master his emotion. He looks at* ANNE-MARIE, *and goes on looking at her as he answers the telephone. His voice sounds almost natural.*]

WOMAN'S VOICE: Were you asleep?

HE: Yes.

WOMAN'S VOICE: Forgive me. I couldn't prevent myself from ringing ... I don't know why, it's idiotic, but I was anxious. What have you been doing?

HE: I went to the cinema, then I went for a stroll ... then I went to bed.

WOMAN'S VOICE: All this divorce business is so painful ... I was anxious. Do forgive me.

HE: Don't go worrying now, there's no need, it's silly.

WOMAN'S VOICE [*after a pause she says what's really on her mind*]: You know, Michel, you didn't have to go. The case could have been heard and decided in your absence. It wouldn't have made any difference. [*Pause.*] Are you there?

HE: Yes.

[ANNE-MARIE *has come a few steps nearer. He still looks at her as the voice on the telephone goes on.*]

WOMAN'S VOICE: I don't want to be a nuisance, Michel, but the thought suddenly hit me ... and I can't get rid of it ... that's why I rang ... to ask you why you went ... Say something, Michel ...

[*He doesn't answer.* ANNE-MARIE *looks at him as though it were she who had to answer. They both try to think of what to say to the woman at the other end of the line.*]

WOMAN'S VOICE: Say something or I shan't be able to sleep. Michel ... Michel ...

HE: To see her again.

[*Silence at the other end. Then the voice resumes.*]

WOMAN'S VOICE: I knew. [*Pause.*] Well?

ANNE-MARIE: Nothing.

HE [*replies in the same tone*]: Nothing.

[*Pause.*]

WOMAN'S VOICE: Are you sure?

HE: Yes. [*Pause.*] Go to sleep now and stop worrying.

WOMAN'S VOICE: ARE YOU QUITE SURE?

HE: Yes.

　　[*Pause.*]

WOMAN'S VOICE: Will you still be coming back tomorrow?

HE [*doesn't reply at once*]: Of course.

　　[*We don't hear the rest of what the voice at the other end says, just* MICHEL NOLLET'S *reply*]: Good night, sleep well.

　　He looks at ANNE-MARIE *as he speaks. He puts down the receiver. Complete anti-climax and depression. Everything terrifyingly upside down. She is still standing, some distance away from him.*]

HE: You said had I any questions to ask you.

SHE: Well ... yes.

HE [*pugnaciously*]: I couldn't bear you to be unfaithful and all the time I was unfaithful myself. Did you know?

SHE: Yes. Valerie used to tell me about your ... adventures.

HE [*as before*]: Didn't you think it was very unfair?

SHE: No, not unfair.

HE: What then?

SHE: Different. Difficult at first and then more and more ... easy ... understandable ... I couldn't tell you, you wouldn't have accepted it.

HE [*is this the real confession*]: You know ... I still can't bear the idea that you didn't want it to happen.

　　[*She doesn't answer. Silence.*]

HE: Did you hear.

SHE: Yes.

HE: What I really came for was to ask you what it was like.

　　[*He laughs.*]

SHE: The same.

HE: Marvellous.

SHE: Yes. Remember. It was the same.

　　[*And once again the telephone starts to ring. Their first impulse is to try to get away, then they stand motionless. We should get the impression that they are hunted, that they cannot go back without once more causing suffering and despair somewhere, and that they are aware of this.*]

OLD LADY: Madame Roche? Just a moment. . . . [*To* MICHEL NOLLET] Monsieur Nollet ... there's someone asking to speak to Madame Roche ... They say it's urgent ... [*She stammers and stutters.*]

HE [*after looking at* ANNE-MARIE]: She's here.

[ANNE-MARIE ROCHE *picks up the receiver.*]

MAN'S VOICE: Anita?

SHE: Yes.

MAN'S VOICE: Forgive me, Anita, I was anxious. It's nothing, just an idiotic anxiety ...

[*Pause.*]

SHE: Where are you?

MAN'S VOICE: On the way there, in a lorry-drivers' café, depressing place ... There's still about another hundred kilometres ... I won't wake you up again ... don't worry ... Anita ...

[MICHEL NOLLET *listens to the conversation, completely transfixed. He finds it very hard to bear what she managed a little while ago. The conversation still goes on.*]

MAN'S VOICE: I love you, Anita ... I can't sleep I'm so ... happy it's all over, this divorce business ... you can't imagine ...

[*Silence. Suddenly she cries out.*]

SHE: Jacques ...

MAN'S VOICE: What is it?

SHE [*recovering*]: Come.

[*Pause.*]

MAN'S VOICE: I'll start now.

[*She hangs up. Pause.*]

SHE: Remember what it was like with that girl, that foreign girl, remember everything exactly. It was the same.

HE [*slowly*]: It's impossible.

SHE: What is?

HE: To accept that.

SHE [*not altogether sincere*]: Was it so marvellous? Really?

HE: Yes. [*Pause.*] Do you understand?

SHE: No.

HE: Do you regret anything?

SHE: No. [*Pause.*] When you say you came to ask me what it was like ... it's not true.

HE: Well ... not entirely ... I came to see you again too, but I knew it would be no use.

SHE: How right you were.

HE: I couldn't even be near you without suffering.
  [*Pause.*]

SHE: What can we do to make these ... memories ... less painful?

HE: Nothing now, I think, the only thing that could have done me any good would have been to kill you, and so ...
  [*They look at each other.*]

HE: I've become just a murderer out of a job ... [*He laughs.*] It's ridiculous.

SHE: Now we're divorced they wouldn't acquit you.

HE: I know. [*He laughs.*] And even if I'd like to kill you I shouldn't like to die for it.
  [*He goes towards her. She draws back.*]

HE: Listen, before this other man comes we still have a little time ...

SHE [*very low, misunderstanding*]: An hour.

HE: Listen ... Would you tell me everything that happened? Everything?

SHE: You want me to try to describe happiness?

HE: Yes. Miserable happiness.

SHE: No. You're making a mistake. You've forgotten the girl in Evreux, so how could you imagine what happened in Paris?

HE: You think I've forgotten?

SHE [*speaking for both of them*]: Yes.
  [*Silence. She goes away from him, leans against the wall, almost as if hiding.*]

SHE [*with great pain but also with an inner joy*]: It doesn't matter about our being together ... now, whether we're together or apart ... it isn't worth making them suffer.

HE: Don't go to America. [*This is the first time he addresses her as 'Tu'.*]

83

[*She doesn't answer.*]

HE [*terrified*]: Don't go. Don't go ... Or else I'll come and live where you are, do you hear? To hell with my work ... I'll come and live in the same town, I'll make your life a misery ... until ...

SHE [*interrupting*]: Until hell starts up all over again?

HE [*raised voice*]: What do you care about hell? [*Pause.*] You either ... [*Pause.*] You don't give a damn about hell either. [*Pause. Entreating.*] Stay in France. So that at least we can meet, even if it's only by chance ... so that it isn't entirely impossible. Let us at least both be in the same country ... otherwise ... it will be unbearable.

[*She doesn't answer.*]

HE [*suddenly desperate*]: We can arrange to meet somewhere in the provinces, out of the way, no one will know ... no one will ever know.

[*They are both filled with anger against things as they are, circumstances.*]

SHE: No. [*She shakes her head.*] No ... no ... to want it, do it deliberately, no ... if we are to meet again, let it be as you were saying before, by chance, as it was with them, with the girl, let's see how chance manages things. [*Crying it out.*] Never otherwise, never again, never again except by chance. ...

HE [*in despair, exhausted, astonished*]: To chuck everything away like that, just because of that trip to Paris, when all the time you were coming back. ...

[*Silence.*]

SHE: He'll be here soon.

HE: I can't leave you.

SHE: We're parted now ... never again except by chance.

HE: What if one of us were dying. ...

SHE: Not even then.

[*Long pause. Their voices change.*]

HE: I don't understand what's happening. [*Pause.*] The beginning and the end are all mixed up ... what can we do so that you and I ... our story [*he smiles*] ... don't just disappear. ...

[*Silence.*]

SHE: The answer is ... nothing ... do nothing ... invent it.

HE: Let love go on growing secretly, in the dark.

SHE: Yes.

HE: Like people kept apart by force of circumstance?

SHE: Yes. Look at me, I'm the only woman now who is forbidden to you.

[*Pause.*]

HE: My wife. [*Long pause.*] Shall we see each other again?

SHE: I don't know.

HE: But if ever, once again, you and I....

SHE: Then we shall probably die, as lovers do.

HE: What is happening?

SHE: When?

HE: Now. The beginning or the end?

SHE: Who knows?

[*Pause.*]

HE: Go and wait for him outside.

SHE [*meekly, making us think of other circumstances*]: Yes.

[*He takes her arm and leads her to the door of the hotel. She is gone. He stands motionless in front of the door, as if he were asleep where he stands.*]

CURTAIN

YUKIO MISHIMA

The Lady Aoi

TRANSLATED FROM THE JAPANESE BY
DONALD KEENE

The Lady Aoi was first performed in Great Britain at the Traverse Theatre in November 1963, with the following cast:

YASUKO ROKUJŌ	Leslie Blacketer
HIKARU WAKABAYASHI	Michael Farnsworth
AOI	Rosamund Dickson
NURSE	Pamela Craig

Directed by TONY HEALEY

A room in a hospital. It is late at night. To stage-right is a large window draped with a curtain. At the back, a bed in which AOI *is sleeping. To the left is a door.*

HIKARU [*enters, led in by the* NURSE. *He wears a raincoat and is carrying a suitcase. He is an unusually good-looking man. He speaks in an undertone*]: She's asleep, isn't she?

NURSE: Yes, she's sound asleep.

HIKARU: It won't waken her if I talk in a normal voice, will it?

NURSE: You can talk a little bit louder if you wish. The medicine is taking effect.

HIKARU [*looking down intently at* AOI's *face*]: How peaceful she looks as she sleeps.

NURSE: Her face looks peaceful enough now.

HIKARU: Now?

NURSE: Yes, but late at night . . .

HIKARU: She's in pain?

NURSE: In terrible pain.

HIKARU [*reading the chart at the foot of the bed*]: 'Aoi Wakaba-yashi. Admitted at 9 p.m. on the 12th.' . . . I wonder if there's anywhere I might spend the night here.

NURSE: Yes. [*She points to the left-rear.*] In the next room.

HIKARU: Is there bedding and all?

NURSE: Yes, there is. Would you like to lie down now?

HIKARU: No, I'll stay up a bit longer. [*He sits on the chair, lights a cigarette.*] I was on a business trip when I got word she was sick. They said it was nothing serious. But when somebody gets put in the hospital it must be serious, mustn't it?

NURSE: Your wife has often had attacks like this, hasn't she?

HIKARU: It's not the first time. But it was a very important business trip. I managed this morning to get through my work and I rushed back as fast as I could. Being away made me worry all the more.

NURSE: I'm sure it did.

[*The telephone on the table tinkles faintly.*]

HIKARU [*lifting the receiver to his ear*]: I can't hear anything.

NURSE: It often rings that way about this time of night.

HIKARU: It's out of order, I suppose. But why should there be a telephone in a hospital room?

NURSE: Every room in this hospital has a telephone.

HIKARU: Who would want to telephone a sick man?

NURSE: It's for the patients' use. There aren't enough nurses to go round, and we ask the patients to call for one on the inside line in case of an emergency. Or, supposing a patient would like a book, he can telephone the bookshop himself. That's on the outside line. We have three operators working twenty-four hours a day in shifts to take care of the outside line. Of course, when patients require absolute quiet, no calls are accepted.

HIKARU: And isn't my wife absolutely quiet?

NURSE: She tosses around a good deal after she falls asleep. She lifts her arms, groans, moves her body from side to side. You really can't say she's absolutely quiet.

HIKARU [*getting angry*]: You mean to say, in this hospital . . .

NURSE: In this hospital we accept no responsibility for the dreams of our patients.

[*Pause. The* NURSE *shows signs of restlessness.*]

HIKARU: What are you so nervous about?

NURSE: It's not necessarily because I've been attracted by you.

HIKARU [*laughing in spite of himself*]: This hospital seems crazier every minute.

NURSE: You're a very good-looking man, you know. A real Prince Genji. But the discipline for nurses in this hospital is terribly strict. We've all been under psychoanalysis, and our sex complexes have all been cleared up. [*She spreads open her arms.*] *All* of them. Things are arranged so we can always satisfy our demands. The director of the hospital and the young doctors are very competent in this respect. Whenever necessary they administer the medicine as prescribed, the medicine known as sex. We never have any trouble with one another.

HIKARU [*impressed*]: You don't say?

NURSE: So, you see, it's perfectly obvious to all of us, without having to make any special analysis, that your wife's dreams all result from sexual complexes. There's nothing for you to worry about. She should be placed under analysis so she can be freed from her complexes. We're giving her the sleep treatment as a first step.

HIKARU: You mean, my wife, with this sleep treatment . . .

NURSE: Yes. [*Still fidgeting.*] That's why I can't have the least of what they call 'understanding' for the patients, or if you'll excuse me, the patients' families or visitors. Don't you agree? Every last one of them is the ghost of a libido. Even that strange visitor who comes here every night . . .

HIKARU: Every night? Here? A visitor?

NURSE: Oh – now I've said it. It's been going on every night, ever since your wife entered the hospital. And it's always late, around this time, because the visitor isn't free any earlier. I've been strictly forbidden to mention it, but it came out before I knew it. . . .

HIKARU: Is it a man – this visitor?

NURSE: Please set your mind at ease – it's a middle-aged woman, a very beautiful one. . . . She'll be coming any minute now. When she arrives I always take advantage of her visit to go out and rest for a while. I don't know why it is, but it makes me feel oddly depressed to be near her.

HIKARU: What sort of woman is she?

NURSE: A very stylishly dressed lady. The upper bourgeoisie – that's the impression she gives. You know, surprisingly enough, it's in bourgeois families that you find the worst sexual repressions. . . . Anyway, she'll be here before long. [*She walks to window at right, raises the curtain.*] Look. There's hardly a house left with its lights burning. All you can see are the two sharp lines of the street lamps. Now is the hour of love. Of loving, of fighting, of hating. When the daytime combat ends, the war by night begins, a gorier, more abandoned struggle. The bugles of the night that proclaim the outbreak of hostilities are sounding now. A woman sheds blood, dies, and comes back to life time and time

again. And she must always die once before she can live.
These men and women who fight wear black badges of
mourning over their weapons. Their flags are all pure white,
but trampled on, wrinkled, and sometimes stained with
blood. The drummer is beating his drum, the drum of the
heart, the drum of honour and shame. . . . How gently they
breathe, they who are about to die. Look at them die,
brazenly flaunting their wounds, the gaping, fatal wounds.
Some men go to death with their faces in the mire. Shame is
the decoration they wear. Look. It's not surprising you
can't see any lights. What lie before you, row on row, as far
as the eye can see, are not houses but graves, foul, putrefied
graves. The light of the moon will never glitter on those
granite slabs. . . . We're angels compared to them. We stand
aloof from the world of love, from the hour of love. All we
do, and that only occasionally, is to produce in bed a
chemical change. No matter how many hospitals like this
there may be, there aren't enough. The director always says
so. . . .

Oh, she's come. She's come! In that car she always rides
in, a big silvery car. It will race here as if it's on wings, and
pull up smartly in front of the hospital. Look! [HIKARU
goes to the window.] It's going over the viaduct now. It always
comes from that direction. There – you see – it's taking the
long way round. . . . Oh, it's here already, in front of the
hospital, before it seems possible. The door of the car has
been opened. I'll be leaving you. Good night. [*She bolts
precipitately from the room by the door to the left. Pause.*]

[*The telephone gives forth a faint, choked tinkle. Pause. From
the door to the left appears the living phantasm of* YASUKO
ROKUJŌ. *She is dressed in Japanese clothes of an expensive cut.
She wears black gloves.*]

HIKARU: Mrs Rokujō!
MRS ROKUJŌ: Hikaru! What a long time it's been, hasn't it?
HIKARU: So it was you, the visitor in the middle of the night.
MRS ROKUJŌ: Who told you about it? [HIKARU *does not
reply.*] It must have been that nurse. She's such a chatterbox.
. . . You know, I've not been coming here to pay a sick-call

– it's been to deliver flowers, every night, on your behalf, ever since I heard you were away.

HIKARU: Flowers?

MRS ROKUJŌ [*opens her hand*]: No, there's nothing in my hands. My flowers are invisible. Flowers of pain is what they are. [*She pretends to arrange flowers at the head of* AOI's *bed.*] These buds I arrange by her pillow will open into ash-coloured blossoms. Many horrible thorns are hidden underneath the leaves, and the flowers themselves exude a loathsome odour that will permeate the room. Look, the peaceful expression drains from her face; the cheeks tremble and are filled with dread. [*She holds her gloved hands over* AOI's *face.*] Aoi is dreaming now that her face has become hideous to look at. The face she had always thought beautiful when she saw it in her mirror has turned into a mass of wrinkles – that is what she dreams. If now I gently touch my hand to her throat [*she touches the sick woman's throat*] Aoi will dream she is being strangled. A rush of blood comes to her face, the breath is choked, her hands and feet writhe in anguish.

HIKARU [*pushing* MRS ROKUJŌ's *hand aside in consternation*]: What are you doing to Aoi?

MRS ROKUJŌ [*moves away. Speaks gently, from a distance*]: I am trying to make her suffer.

HIKARU: Excuse me, but Aoi is my wife, and I won't permit you to bother her any further. Please be so good as to leave.

MRS ROKUJŌ [*even gentler*]: I will not leave.

HIKARU: What do you –

MRS ROKUJŌ [*approaches and gently takes* HIKARU's *hand*]: I came tonight because I wanted to see you.

HIKARU [*wrests away his hand*]: Your hand is like ice.

MRS ROKUJŌ: That's not surprising. There's no blood in it.

HIKARU: Those gloves of yours ...

MRS ROKUJŌ: If you dislike my gloves I'll remove them. Nothing could be simpler. [*She slips off her gloves as she walks across the room, and puts them next to the telephone.*] At any rate, I have business, important business, that must be disposed of. That's why I have been running about this way – don't think it hasn't been a nuisance – in the middle of the night. The middle of the night . . . [*She looks at her wristwatch.*] It's already after one. The night is not like the day, it's free. All things, people and inanimate objects alike, sleep. This wall, the chest of drawers, the window panes, the door – all of them are asleep. And while they sleep they're full of cracks and crevices – it's no problem to pass through them. When you pass through a wall not even the wall is aware of it. What do you suppose night is? Night is when all things are in harmony. By day light and shadow war, but with nightfall the night inside the house holds hands with the night outside the house. They are the same thing. The night air is party to the conspiracy. Hate and love, pain and joy: everything and anything join hands in the night air. The murderer in the dark, I am sure, feels affection for the woman he has killed. [*Laughs.*] What is it? Why do you stare at me that way? You must be shocked to see what an old woman I've become.

HIKARU: I thought you swore never to see me again.

MRS ROKUJŌ: You were very happy to hear me make that vow. Then you married Aoi. [*She turns fiercely to the sleeping* AOI.] This weak, sickly woman! [*Emptily*] Since then every night has been sleepless. Even when I shut my eyes I have not slept. I have not slept a wink since then.

HIKARU: Have you come here to be pitied by me?

MRS ROKUJŌ: I really don't know myself why I've come. When I feel I want to kill you, I must be thinking that I'd like to be pitied by your dead self. And amidst feelings of every sort, simultaneously, there is myself. Isn't it strange that I should be present at the same time with all those different existences?

HIKARU: I don't understand what you're talking about.

MRS ROKUJŌ [*lifting her face to his*]: Kiss me.

HIKARU: Stop it, please.

MRS ROKUJŌ: Your beautiful eyebrows, your terrifyingly clear eyes, your cold nose, your –

HIKARU: Stop it, please.

MRS ROKUJŌ: – your lips. [*She kisses him quickly.*]

HIKARU [*jumping back*]: Stop it, please, I say.

MRS ROKUJŌ: The first time I kissed you, too, you shied away like a deer, just as you did now.

HIKARU: Yes, I did. I wasn't particularly in love with you. All I had was a childish curiosity. You took advantage of it. I suppose you've learned now the punishment a woman gets for taking advantage of a man's curiosity.

MRS ROKUJŌ: You were not the least in love. You studied me. That, at least, was your intent, wasn't it? How adorable you were! I hope you'll always stay that way!

HIKARU: I'm not a child any more. I am in fact the head of a household. Have you no sense of shame? That's my wife who's sleeping there next to you.

MRS ROKUJŌ: My only purpose in coming here has been to dispose of my business. I have nothing to be ashamed of.

HIKARU: What business have you?

MRS ROKUJŌ: To be loved by you.

HIKARU: Are you in your right mind, Mrs Rokujō?

MRS ROKUJŌ: My name is Yasuko.

HIKARU: I am not obliged to call you by your first name.

MRS ROKUJŌ [*suddenly kneels, throws her arms around* HIKARU'*s knees, and rubs her cheek against them*]: I beg you, please don't be so cold to me.

HIKARU: This is the first time I've ever seen you lose your pride so. [*To himself*] It's funny. It doesn't feel as if a human being were holding me, and yet I can't move my feet.

MRS ROKUJŌ: I had no pride, from the very beginning.

HIKARU: You should have confessed it earlier. Perhaps things might have lasted awhile longer.

MRS ROKUJŌ: It was your fault not to have realized it. Couldn't you tell that my eyes had long since lost their pride? The clearest sign that a woman has lost her pride is when she talks in a high-handed way. A woman longs to be a queen because a queen has the most pride to lose. . . . Ah, your knees — your knees are a cold, hard pillow.

HIKARU: Yasuko . . .

MRS ROKUJŌ: I could sleep on this pillow. A cold, hard pillow that would never get warm. . . . My pillow becomes scalding hot as soon as my head touches it, and my head spends the night fleeing from the pillow's heat to the cold. A man who could walk barefoot over burning desert sands could not tread on my pillow.

HIKARU [*somewhat gentler*]: Please be careful. I am a very weak man when my pity is aroused.

MRS ROKUJŌ: Now I understand! You married Aoi out of pity too! Didn't you?

HIKARU [*pushing her aside*]: Don't jump to any conclusions like that. [*He sits on the chair.* MRS ROKUJŌ *still clings to his legs and rubs her cheek against his knees like a cat.*]

MRS ROKUJŌ: Please don't abandon me.

HIKARU [*smoking*]: You were abandoned long ago.

MRS ROKUJŌ: You still love me.

HIKARU: Did you come here to tell me that? [*Teasingly*] I thought you said you came to torture Aoi.

MRS ROKUJŌ: I was aiming to kill two birds with one stone. Give me a cigarette, please. [HIKARU *offers her one, but* MRS ROKUJŌ *snatches the half-smoked cigarette from* HIKARU'*s mouth and puffs at it.* HIKARU, *at a loss what else to do, puts the cigarette he had offered her into his mouth and lights it.*]

HIKARU: In those days I was unstable, shaky on my feet. I wanted to be chained. I wanted a cage to shut me in. You were that cage. Then, when I wished to be free again, you were still a cage, a chain.

MRS ROKUJŌ: I loved to look at your eyes, those eyes searching for freedom inside the cage that was myself, the chain that was myself. That was when I first really fell in love with you. It was autumn, the beginning of autumn. You had come to visit me at my house on the lake. I went to meet you in my sailboat, as far as the yacht harbour next to the station. ... It was a wonderfully clear day. The mast was creaking gently. The boat ...

HIKARU: The sail above the boat ...

MRS ROKUJŌ [*with sudden asperity*]: Don't you find it disagreeable to share the same memories with me?

HIKARU: They're not the same. We happen to have been together, that's all.

MRS ROKUJŌ: But it was the same boat. The sail was flapping madly above us. Oh, if that sail were here again! If only it stood over us again!

HIKARU [*staring at the window*]: Is that it coming from out there?

MRS ROKUJŌ: It's come!

[*Weird music. From the right a large sailboat glides onstage. It moves forward with the deliberation of a swan, and halts between them and the bed, where it stands like a screen shielding the bed.* HIKARU *and* MRS ROKUJŌ *act as if they were aboard the boat.*]

MRS ROKUJŌ: We're on the lake!

HIKARU: A wonderful breeze!

MRS ROKUJŌ: This is the first time you've come to my country house, isn't it? It's on the side of the lake below the mountain. Soon you'll be able to see the roof, behind that clump of trees. It's a pale-green roof. Foxes prowl around the house when it gets dark, you know, and you can hear them yelping in the mountains. Have you ever heard a fox's cries?

HIKARU: No, never.

MRS ROKUJŌ: Tonight you'll hear them. And the shrieks that a chicken lets out before it dies, when a fox is ripping its throat.

HIKARU: I'd just as soon not hear such things.

MRS ROKUJŌ: I'm sure you'll like my garden, I'm sure of it. In the spring parsley grows along the borders of the lawn and fills the garden with the most delicious scent. Then, when the spring rains fall, the garden becomes submerged and completely disappears. You can see the hydrangea blossoms drowning as the water creeps up through the grass. Have you ever seen a drowned hydrangea? It's autumn now and swarms of tiny insects will be flying up from the reeds in the garden to skim over the surface of the lake, like sleds on the ice.

HIKARU: That's your house over there, isn't it?

MRS ROKUJŌ: Yes, the one with the pale-green roof. You can tell it from much farther off in the evening, because of the sunset. The roof and the windows sparkle, and the light is

like a beacon that tells from afar where the house is. [*Pause.*]
What's the matter? You're not saying a word.

HIKARU [*gently*]: There's no need to say anything.

MRS ROKUJŌ: It's medicine to me to hear you talk that way,
a medicine that cures all my wounds in an instant, a marvellous medicine. But I know the kind of person you are – you
give the medicine first and only afterward inflict the wound.
You never do it the other way. First the medicine, after the
medicine the wound, and after the wound no more medicine
... I understand well enough. I'm already an old woman.
Once I get wounded I won't recover quickly like a girl. I
tremble with fright whenever you say anything affectionate.
I wonder what horrible wound awaits me after so efficacious
a medicine. Of late, the less affectionate you talk the happier
it makes me.

HIKARU: You seem convinced that you're going to suffer.

MRS ROKUJŌ: Pain comes, as night follows the day, sooner or
later.

HIKARU: I can't believe I have the strength to cause anybody
pain.

MRS ROKUJŌ: That's because you're young. One of these days
you will wake up in the morning with nothing on your mind,
and while you are out walking with your dog, perhaps, you
will suddenly become aware that dozens of women somewhere, unseen by you, are suffering, and you will understand
that the very fact you are alive is in itself a cause of suffering
to many women. Even though you can't see them, they can
see you, and it is useless for you to turn your eyes away, for
you are as plainly visible as a castle that rises on a height over
a city.

HIKARU: Why don't we drop the subject?

MRS ROKUJŌ: Yes, let's. As long as I can still talk about such
things I should count myself lucky.

HIKARU: I can see your house very clearly now – the lattice-
work of the second-floor windows, the wooden railing of
the balcony. There's nobody at home, is there?

MRS ROKUJŌ: No, the house is empty. That's where I'd like
to live with you until I die.

HIKARU: Until you die? You shouldn't talk of such uncertainties. Who knows – we may die tomorrow. Supposing, for example, the boat capsized ...

MRS ROKUJŌ: The boat capsized! I wonder why I didn't buy a boat for you which would instantly capsize? Obviously I hadn't my wits about me.

HIKARU [*shaking the mast*]: Look! It's going to turn over!
    [MRS ROKUJŌ *throws her arms around* HIKARU. *They embrace.*]

AOI'S VOICE [*faintly, from the distance*]: Help! Help!
    [*As her voice is heard, the shadow of* AOI, *writhing on her sickbed with her arms thrust out, appears on the sail.*]

HIKARU: Wasn't that a voice somewhere just now?

MRS ROKUJŌ: No, it must have been a fox. In the daytime, when the lake is still, you can hear the fox yelps gliding over the water, all the way from the mountain.

HIKARU: I can't hear it any more.

MRS ROKUJŌ: I wonder why there must be a left and a right to everything. Now I am standing by your right side. That means your heart is far away. But if I move to your left side I won't be able to see your right profile.

HIKARU: The only thing for me to do is to turn into a gas and evaporate.

MRS ROKUJŌ: Yes. When I am on your right I am jealous of everything to your left. I feel as if someone surely is sitting there.

HIKARU [*makes the motions of leaning over the side of the boat and dipping his hand in the water*]: The lake's the only thing sitting on my left. What a cold hand it has! ... Look at that! [*He shows her his wet hand.*] It's almost frozen. And it's only the beginning of autumn.
    [*There is a groan behind the sail.*]

HIKARU: What was that?

MRS ROKUJŌ: What?

HIKARU: I couldn't hear. It sounded as if someone were groaning.

MRS ROKUJŌ [*listens intently*]: It's the creaking of the mast.

HIKARU: The wind has shifted, hasn't it? [*He makes the*

gestures of manipulating the sail.] I see the reeds on the shore plainly now, bending in the wind. The wind is shaking spasms over the surface of the lake.

MRS ROKUJŌ: Yes, isn't it? . . . I was just thinking that, if you fell in love with some woman much younger and prettier than I, and you married her . . .

HIKARU: Yes?

MRS ROKUJŌ: I don't think I would die.

HIKARU [*laughs*]: That's fine.

MRS ROKUJŌ: I wouldn't die, but I think I would certainly kill her. My spirit would leave my body even while I was still alive, and it would go to torture her. My living ghost would afflict her and torment her and torture her, and it would not cease until it killed her. She, poor creature, would die haunted night after night by an evil spirit.

AOI'S VOICE [*faintly, from the distance*]: Help! Help!

HIKARU: That voice again. What can it be?

MRS ROKUJŌ: It's just the sail flapping in the wind. It's the sound of the wind.

[*The shadow-image of* AOI *thrusting out her arms in anguish is clearly projected on the sail.*]

AOI'S VOICE [*fairly loudly this time*]: Ah-h! Ah-h! Help! Help!

HIKARU [*aghast*]: I'm sure I heard a voice.

MRS ROKUJŌ: It was the shriek of a chicken whose windpipe was gnawed by a fox. The wind carried it here from the shore. That shows how close we are.

HIKARU: I wonder if someone isn't drowning.

MRS ROKUJŌ: Drowning? Who would be drowning? If anyone's drowning, it's us!

AOI'S VOICE [*clearly*]: Help! Help!

HIKARU: It's Aoi!

MRS ROKUJŌ [*laughs*]: No, it's a chicken.

HIKARU: I'm sure it's Aoi's voice.

MRS ROKUJŌ: Don't leave me!

HIKARU: You're impossible! You've been torturing Aoi.

MRS ROKUJŌ: No, it's not my fault. It's your –
   [AOI'S VOICE: *groans.*]

HIKARU: Aoi!

MRS ROKUJŌ: Try to get hold of yourself! You're not in love with Aoi. Look at me. Make no mistake. You're in love with me. With me.

HIKARU [*shakes his head*]: No, I am not.

[*The two confront each other in silence. Weird music.* MRS ROKUJŌ *turns from* HIKARU *and attempts to pass behind the sail.* HIKARU *stops her.* MRS ROKUJŌ *twists herself free and disappears behind the sail.* HIKARU *follows her. The stage becomes dark. Amidst weird music the sailboat slowly moves offstage to the left. When it is no longer visible the stage becomes light again.* MRS ROKUJŌ *is not to be seen.* HIKARU *stands alone in apparent stupefaction.*]

HIKARU [*as if struck by a sudden thought, he picks up the telephone receiver on the desk*]: Hello, hello. Yes. Outside line, please. ... Is this outside? Please give me Nakano 999.... Hello. Is that Mr Rokujō's house? May I speak to Yasuko? Yes, Mrs Rokujō.... She retired some time ago? Yes? In her bedroom? ... I'm sorry, it can't be helped. Please wake her. Tell her Hikaru is calling. It's urgent. Please wake her. Yes....

[*Pause.* HIKARU *looks anxiously at* AOI's *bed. She is sleeping peacefully in a supine position.*]

HIKARU: Hello, hello ... Is that you, Yasuko? What? Have you been at home all evening? You've been asleep? This *is* Yasuko I'm talking with, isn't it? [*To himself*] Yes, the voice is certainly hers.... Then what I saw was a living ghost. ... Yes, hello, hello.

[*There is a knock on the door to the left.*]

MRS ROKUJŌ'S VOICE [*from outside the door. She speaks very distinctly*]: Hikaru, I've forgotten something. I forgot my gloves. My black gloves, next to the telephone. Do you see them? Please get them for me.

[HIKARU *distractedly picks up the black gloves and, leaving the receiver off the hook, walks to the door to the left. He opens the door and goes out. As soon as* HIKARU *leaves,* MRS ROKUJŌ's *voice on the telephone suddenly becomes loud enough for the audience to hear.*]

MRS ROKUJŌ'S VOICE [*from the telephone*]: Hello. Hello ...

What is it, Hikaru? What's the matter? You wake me up in the middle of the night, and then suddenly you don't say a word. What do you want? Why don't you answer? ... Hello, Hikaru, hello, hello ...

[*At the last 'hello' from the telephone,* AOI *thrusts out her arms at the telephone and with a horrible cry collapses over the bed and dies. The stage immediately blacks out.*]

CURTAIN

CECIL TAYLOR

Allergy

All inquiries concerning performing rights, professional or amateur, readings or any other use of
this material should be directed to the author's
agent: Beatrice Narizzano, Barry Krost Asso-
ciates Limited, 45 Clarges Street, London w1.

Allergy was first performed at the Traverse Theatre in January 1966, with the following cast:

JIM,   David Strong
      Editor of Socialist Reflection,
      organ of the New Socialist Party.

CHRISTOPHER,   Heinz Bernard
      Second reporter on the Clydesdale
      Courant *and main contributor –*
      under a nom-de-plume, for safety
     – to Socialist Reflection.

BARBARA, *Regular contributor to the*   Kate Binchy
      Daily Worker *Fighting Fund.*

Directed by MICHAEL GELIOT

Late afternoon. Spring. A room in a cottage in Ross. The few items of furniture look as if they've been lifted from a rubbish dump. In the centre – an island in a sea of empty beer cans – is a table. At one corner, New Socialism's *printing press – an ancient duplicator – stands, primed for the next edition. A curtain of sacking stretches across part of the room, screening a crude shower. The whitewashed walls are relieved by pages cut from the colour supplements, action paintings and political posters:* 'Drink Coca-Cola!' 'Yanks get out of Holy Loch!' 'No Yanks in Vietnam!' 'Yanks go home!' 'Hands off Dominica!' *and other such pious sentiments.*

> [JIM, *in a dirty, grease-stained, brick red, Marks and Spencer's dressing-gown is having an argument with his tape recorder.*]

TAPE RECORDER: You're absolutely sure about this Chip Machine?

JIM: I'm telling you! The Great Exhibition. Ibrox Park. 193 ... 37.

TAPE RECORDER: I can find no reference to it in current periodicals.

JIM: You put your threepence into the machine – and out came a bag of chips. But if you ask me, the whole thing was a bloody swindle.

TAPE RECORDER: Explain yourself.

JIM: In the front ... you see? was this machine. But at the back, they'd have a room fitted out like a fish and chip shop. You'd put your threepenny bit in the slot. A girl would catch it. Shout: threepenny bag, to the fryer. The fryer'd shout back: threepenny bag coming up! The girl –

TAPE RECORDER: I can't accept this!

JIM: What can't you accept?

TAPE RECORDER: I cannot accept that a fraud of that nature –

JIM: You can't accept anything!

TAPE RECORDER [*continuing*]: Would be allowed –

JIM: I'm telling you! You're a total write-off!

TAPE RECORDER: At an international exhibition –

JIM: A total, dead, hopeless, utter, futile loss!

TAPE RECORDER: No need to get offensive!

JIM [*switching off the machine*]: Oh, go'n' fuck yourself, will you!
[*He sits down at the typewriter on the table, types a few rapid sentences, then pulls the sheet of paper from the machine to read.*]

JIM [*reading*]: 'Circulation!' sneers the current *Socialist Reflection* editorial, commenting on *New Socialism*, 'Thrombosis' would be a more apt expression!
While admiring the wit, we can hardly applaud the accuracy. *New Socialism* has a circulation of 200 copies per month which compares more than favourably with *Socialist Reflection*'s admitted 150 ... We mention those figures –
[*Breaks off, throws the editorial down to rummage through the sea of empty beer cans for a full one, tossing the empties against the wall in frustration.*

He finally finds a full one, takes a three-inch nail from his dressing-gown pocket and a hammer from the table drawer, and hammers two holes in the can. He saturates himself with the spray ... wipes his face with the bottom of his dressing-gown and settles down to study his editorial, making corrections from time to time with his pen. He breaks off at the sound of a car drawing up outside, goes to the window, peers out, then quickly returns to his typewriter, putting a fresh sheet in the machine and typing away at breakneck speed.

He types away, pretending to be so occupied that he doesn't notice the entrance of CHRISTOPHER *and* BARBARA. *Looks up with pretended surprise but is visibly shaken by* BARBARA. *He sits, taking in her legs, her hips and her breasts.* CHRISTOPHER *is struggling with a case.*

BARBARA *stands, enjoying the appreciation.*

CHRISTOPHER *has a bandage round his head and from time to time, during the conversation that follows, keeps scratching himself and moving about restlessly.*]

CHRISTOPHER: You haven't gone to press yet?

JIM: Just doing a biting editorial, annihilating Libberman. Who's the woman?

CHRISTOPHER: Good. I've brought some notes countering his distortions on The Permanent Revolution.

JIM [*to* BARBARA]: I've no food in the house, you know? If you want something to eat, you'll have to drive into Ullapool and pick it up. I'm down to Velveeta and unleavened bread.

BARBARA: Unleavened bread?

JIM: Keeps better. Brought a case of it, when I came up here.

BARBARA: Oh, we've brought loads of food! Steak ... Tins of asparagus ... anchovies ... goulash.

JIM [*to* CHRISTOPHER]: Who is she?

BARBARA: Tins of champignons. [JIM *looks puzzled.*] Tiny mushrooms ... for toast ... or chicken ...

CHRISTOPHER [*to* BARBARA]: We bought a couple of tins of whole chicken, too, didn't we ... ?

JIM [*to* BARBARA]: You planning to stay here?

BARBARA [*putting her hands out to* CHRISTOPHER *and drawing him, amorously, to her*]: If you don't mind. We'd love to.

CHRISTOPHER: We won't interfere with your work, Jim. I can guarantee you that. I've got a heavy programme myself.

BARBARA [*to* JIM]: And I can type.

CHRISTOPHER [*to* JIM]: She'll be a great help.

JIM [*with no great enthusiasm*]: There's a room ...

CHRISTOPHER [*to* JIM]: She can work a duplicator.

JIM [*to* BARBARA]: What's he done with Pat and the kids?

CHRISTOPHER [*to* JIM]: Hardly 'kids', Jim ... twelve and fourteen. ... At that age ... they're ... absolutely emotionally independent. You can hardly call them 'kids'!

BARBARA: We've brought our own bedding.

CHRISTOPHER: And air beds ...

BARBARA: Double air beds ... Did you know they actually make air beds double, Jim?

JIM: What did he do with Pat?

BARBARA [*seized by a sudden idea*]: Do you know what we can do in the morning, darling? Take them into the garden ... Lie in the morning sun, breathing in the scent of the bog myrtle and the sea ... Listening to the birds ... and the cuckoo ...

JIM: Bit early for the cuckoo, hen.

CHRISTOPHER [*to* BARBARA]: The mornings are reserved for creative writing, dear. Remember?

JIM: Have you nowhere else you can go? I can't keep you.
That's definite ... What happened to his head? – I'm just
surviving ... I'm making no sacrifices for any bugger!
Friends or no friends ... I've got 900 odd quid to get this
Twentieth Century Marxism – An Enquiry out ... At three
quid a week, that gives me six years ... I should just make
it ...

BARBARA: You don't need to worry about us, Jim. We're
going to be completely self-supporting. I'm going to put an
advert in the *New Statesman* for typing work and Christopher's going to write book reviews and articles ...

CHRISTOPHER: In the afternoon. In the morning, I've got
my creative writing ... Jim, I've got a fantastic idea.

BARBARA: It's wonderful! About a man who goes out to
challenge society.

CHRISTOPHER: To the absolute limit.

BARBARA: He goes out into a remote part of Scotland ...

JIM: Christopher?

BARBARA: And he occupies a piece of land.

CHRISTOPHER: I'm not clear yet, whether he should build a
fence round it or not. I'll have to let that problem simmer in
my subconscious a bit.

JIM: Barbed wire or electric?

CHRISTOPHER: I don't know.

JIM: If you had the fence ... and the book was filmed ...

BARBARA: It would never be filmed ... It's too devastating an
indictment of the System.

JIM: Well ... if it was ...

BARBARA: In Soviet Russia, maybe ...

JIM: That would always be some action ... wouldn't it? For
the film ... Him building the fence ...

BARBARA: You should put that letter to your boss into it,
darling ... especially the part where you say something
about your action not being wise ...

CHRISTOPHER [*quoting*]: 'I know what I am doing is probably
not a wise action ... It isn't. I could fail. I'm going into this
with the near certainty of failure in front of me all the
time.'

BARBARA: Darling, you won't fail. I know ...

JIM [*to* BARBARA]: What's he going to fail at?

CHRISTOPHER: I'm getting near forty.

BARBARA: You don't look anything like forty!

JIM: Do *I*?

BARBARA [*not in the least interested*]: It's difficult to say.

JIM: I am. Forty-two.

CHRISTOPHER [*bringing out the letter*]: 'I must take this decisive step now – or never. If I fail – I fail ... But if I did not take this step, I know that I would spend the rest of my life regretting not taking it.'

BARBARA: Darling, I thought you said you'd left the letter on the editor's desk ...

CHRISTOPHER: Yes ... Well ... I thought I'd better do one more draft ... To make sure I was expressing what I wanted to say with absolute accuracy ...

BARBARA [*looking at him suspiciously*]: Oh ...

CHRISTOPHER: You see ... This theme I'm tackling ... It's so big ... I'm inviting failure...

BARBARA: Darling ... You're not going to fail. I know it ... I have faith in you ...

CHRISTOPHER: There's no certainty about creative writing, dear ... You can't say what's going to happen ... You just don't know ... [*Scratching.*]

JIM: What's the matter with you? Got fleas?

CHRISTOPHER: Probably a reaction to my head ...

JIM: What happened to his head?

BARBARA [*going to nurse* CHRISTOPHER]: You know what we're going to do, darling? We're going to have a nice dinner ... with wine ... We'll organize our bedroom ... And have a nice, early night ... You've had a very hard day, darling ... [*Kissing him*] Won't that be nice, dearest?

CHRISTOPHER [*to* JIM]: The first-aid box fell on me, taking a hairpin bend.

JIM: That's asking for trouble – a first-aid box in a car.

CHRISTOPHER [*sharply*]: Jim. Is that very Marxist of you?

JIM: If it hadn't been there, it wouldn't 've fallen on your head, for Christ's sake!

BARBARA: At least we had something to dress his head with, when it did fall.

JIM: If it hadn't been there, for Christ's sake! it wouldn't have fallen – and you wouldn't have needed it to dress his head!

CHRISTOPHER [*quoting*]: 'If 'is a totally useless instrument in the study of history.

BARBARA: It's a fabulous first-aid box! *Everything*'s in it! Bandages, iodine, splints . . . And a gorgeous pair of surgical scissors!

CHRISTOPHER [*scratching himself, and looking more and more worried*]: I could've been hit by any of the twenty odd boxes and cases in the car.

BARBARA [*anxiously*]: Darling . . . Are you sure you're all right . . .

CHRISTOPHER: I'm fine, dear . . .

BARBARA: Les once broke a bone in his arm in an accident . . . and drove all the way home from Pitlochry without realizing it . . .

JIM: Les?

BARBARA: My husband. [CHRISTOPHER *suddenly makes to go out.*] Where are you going, darling?

CHRISTOPHER [*rushing out*]: Just going to get something from the car.

BARBARA [*following him with her eyes*]: Hasn't Christopher beautiful hair?

JIM: All right. What about mine?

BARBARA: Maybe if you combed it . . .

JIM: I have a shower three times a day. Look! [*Opens his dressing-gown.*] What about that shining body? Eh?

BARBARA [*her interest roused by the display of hairy, virile chest*]: You've got a massive chest!

JIM: I'm a big boy, hen . . . [BARBARA *goes over to unpack a case of food*] Did you bring any tomato soup? That's what I fancy for dinner . . . Tomato soup . . . and thick, buttered rolls . . .

BARBARA: We just brought packets to save space . . . Gorgeous continental recipes . . . Liver with meat balls . . . Austrian fish soup . . . salami . . . broth with dumplings . . .

[CHRISTOPHER *enters white and shaken.*] Christopher, darling
... Did you notice any tomato in the packets we bought ...

CHRISTOPHER: No.

BARBARA: Darling, have you masses of hair on your chest
like Jimmy? [*Makes to open his shirt. He resists.*] Let me see,
darling ...

CHRISTOPHER [*keeping his hands on his chest*]: Yes. I have. [*He
collapses on a chair.*]

BARBARA: It doesn't matter if you haven't, darling ... I don't
mind, one way or the other ... Are you as tall as Jim?
Christopher, darling ... Stand up a minute ... [CHRISTO-
PHER *rises weakly.*] Stand back to back ... Umh ... nearly ...
You're a big, strong boy, too ... [CHRISTOPHER *sinks
back into the chair.*] And all that beautiful manhood wasted
... for how long, darling ... [CHRISTOPHER *sunk into himself ... brooding over some problem.*] How long, Christopher ...
What's the matter, darling ... Is it your head?

CHRISTOPHER: I'm fine ... I'm fine ... What did you
say?

JIM: How long was the beautiful manhood wasted?

CHRISTOPHER: Eh?

JIM: On Pat.

CHRISTOPHER: I was married at twenty ...

JIM: Promoted to second reporter on *Clydesdale Courant* ...
and bought a car ... Couldn't live with his life incomplete.
Got wife, a semi, and babies ...

BARBARA [*looking at* CHRISTOPHER]: He must have been
beautiful at twenty!

JIM: You should've seen me! I was an athlete.

BARBARA: Oh ...

JIM: Used to climb Ben Lomond stripped to the waist in winter. Sunbathing all summer. Turning down homo proposi-
tions twice a day!

BARBARA: I think everybody has the right to express their
love and sexuality in whatever way they want to ... [JIM *is
rummaging for more beer.*]

JIM: Christ! I haven't emptied them all yet!

BARBARA: Why don't you throw out the empties, after you've

finished with them? Then you'd have no bother finding the full ones.

JIM: Kicks. [*More searching.*] Bloody hell!

BARBARA [*rising*]: I'll go and get you something really nice to drink. Out of this world! [*She makes to go.*]

CHRISTOPHER: You can manage yourself, dear?

BARBARA [*going*]: You just sit there and gather your strength, baby ...

JIM: I'm going to have a shower. That woman excites me!

CHRISTOPHER [*in a panic*]: Jim! I've got to get out of this! For Christ's sake!

JIM: I've got to have a shower, man!

CHRISTOPHER: Just give me one minute, Jim. Please. Listen to me.

JIM: I can listen to you in my shower. [*Going behind the curtain.*] If you want to stay here, you'll have to discipline yourself not to interfere in my way of life.

CHRISTOPHER: I've got to get out of here, Jim. I'm in – [*Breaks off, at* BARBARA *returning.*]

BARBARA: You've locked the boot, darling. [CHRISTOPHER *hands her the keys. She goes out.*]

CHRISTOPHER [*going up to the shower*]: Jim. I'm in a jam. What am I going to do? I've got to get out of here. For Christ's sake! Put that bloody shower off! Listen to me ...

JIM: It's great! Like a mountain spring! You can have one yourself, later.

CHRISTOPHER: She's expecting me to sleep with her tonight.

JIM: Lusting, man. Not expecting. Bloody lusting! I'm not jealous. But you've got to admit you're totally unworthy! Seriously.

CHRISTOPHER: It's out of the question, Jim. I can't do it. It's impossible. I can't ... Jim, what am I going to do?

BARBARA [*bringing in a Winchester of alcohol*]: Christopher, darling ... Where did you put the fruit juice? It's not in the boot.

CHRISTOPHER: One of the cartons in the back.

BARBARA: Oh ... Where's Jim?

JIM: In here. Having a shower. Coming in with me?

BARBARA: Oh ... That's marvellous! You've a shower! I was worried about the bathing facilities.

JIM: Fed from a mountain burn ... All the way down from the hills ...

BARBARA: Oh, that's gorgeous! Isn't that gorgeous, darling ... [*Going out.*]

JIM [*coming out of his shower. Pointing to the Winchester*]: What the hell's she got there?

CHRISTOPHER: Alcohol. Gallons. Half-a-boot-full! It's all right. I was worried at first it was that stuff that made you blind. But it's pure alcohol.

JIM: Where'd she get it from?

CHRISTOPHER: She worked in a chemist's shop, Jim. She'll be back –

JIM: She been knocking off stuff from the shop? Look! I'm not getting involved with the police for receiving stolen –

CHRISTOPHER: It's all right. She's faked the stock books. Jim ... She'll be back in a minute ... I've never been in such a desperate position in my life. She's been looking forward to sleeping with me for months!

JIM: Christ! Have you not given it to her yet?

CHRISTOPHER: You know my principles, Jim.

JIM: Beats me she hasn't had your trousers off on the way up!

CHRISTOPHER [*forgetting his problem, in his pride in the conquest*]: Yes! She's got a right passion for me, hasn't she?

JIM: The secret is, boy ... not to worry about it. Montaigne had the same problem from time to time ... and Boswell ... Just relax and don't think about it ... and it'll soon be springing to attention again, smarter than ever!

CHRISTOPHER: It's nothing to do with potency, Jim. I happen to be very strongly sexed ... Extremely potent ... The problem's bigger than that, Jim. [*Opening his shirt and displaying a mass of ugly, red blotches covering his chest*] Look!

JIM: Christ! What is it? [*Drawing back.*] Is it infectious?

CHRISTOPHER: It's all over me ... From tip to toe ...

BARBARA [*returning with a case of fruit juice*]: Chicken or goulash for dinner?

JIM: Chicken, please ...

[*She goes out again.*]

CHRISTOPHER: I had this itch all the way from Spean Bridge ...

JIM: Let's see it again. Christ! Put you off your meat!

CHRISTOPHER: That's why I went outside before ... To check what was causing it. You know what it is, don't you?

JIM: Scarlet fever.

CHRISTOPHER: It's happened to me before ... Not so bad as this ... But that time I was doing a story on the Blantyre Beauty Queen ... And she got me to come up to her house, while her husband was out at work, one afternoon ...

JIM: God! They never chase me like that. I've got to work hard for my micks!

CHRISTOPHER: She was sitting there, with her skirt up ... You know? Waiting for it ... And this itch started ... I went into the bedroom – and I found this rash.

BARBARA [*enters with a case of food*]: By the way, it's *diabetic* fruit juice ... But it's gorgeous ... [*Goes out again.*]

CHRISTOPHER: I've had slight attacks when I even started getting ideas ... One of the girls in the office ... Long, red hair ... combed straight down ... You know what it is. It's an allergy.

JIM: To women?

CHRISTOPHER: To adultery.

JIM: Impossible.

CHRISTOPHER: I'm telling you.

JIM: Is it all over your body?

CHRISTOPHER [*lifting his trouser leg*]: Right down. Look. The idea of stripping in front of her.

JIM: Nasty ... [*Pause.*] What about you getting into bed before her?

CHRISTOPHER: Worse. When she does see it!

JIM: And feel it ... Bad!

CHRISTOPHER: She's not to know it's an allergy. She'll think I'm diseased.

JIM [*checking*]: You're not diseased?

CHRISTOPHER: It's an allergy, I'm telling you.

JIM: Explain to her, then. Tell her.

CHRISTOPHER: I've been watching myself. Every time she's come near me, since I've found out ... She doesn't raise a flicker in me ... Not a spark ... You can imagine what a disaster I'd be in bed with her.

JIM: And after getting her all worked up.

CHRISTOPHER: What am I going to do, Jim?

BARBARA [*coming in with a carton of chocolate*]: Diabetic chocolate. Anybody want a bar?

JIM [*taking one*]: Thanks. Be a change from unleavened bread. [*Takes the Winchester and makes to pour out a cup.*]

BARBARA: You don't drink it neat. I'm going to fix it for you. Have you a big jug ... or a basin ...

JIM: Under the sink. [*She goes over and brings out an ancient enamel basin.*] Big enough?

BARBARA: Fine.

JIM [*to* CHRISTOPHER]: I sometimes use it for a pee, when it's too wet to go outside ...

BARBARA: That's all right. I'll rinse it out.

CHRISTOPHER: For Christ's sake, Barbara! The bacteria!

JIM: The alcohol'll kill them.

CHRISTOPHER: Preserve them – not kill them. Alcohol preserves!

BARBARA: Darling, it won't kill us.

CHRISTOPHER [*to* JIM]: You're having us on, Jim. You don't pee in that, do you?

JIM: I don't know ... I'm not sure ... Sometimes ... probably ... I wash it out ... I mix oatmeal in it and make unleavened bannocks ...

BARBARA [*with a tin of fruit juice*]: Where's your tin-opener, Jim?

JIM [*handing her his nail*]: Here. Just hammer the nail into the can – either side.

CHRISTOPHER: Oh, God! Imagine the bacteria crowding on that bloody nail! Probably been in his filthy pocket since he came here!

BARBARA: We'll go to Ullapool in the morning, darling, and pick up a tin-opener.

CHRISTOPHER [*seizing a chance to escape*]: Look ... We can't do without a tin-opener ... I'll run over to Ullapool now ... while –

BARBARA: No, darling ... You're going to sit down and rest.

JIM [*to* CHRISTOPHER]: And gather your strength. Don't worry. I'm thinking ...

BARBARA: Thinking?

JIM: About Boswell ... You ever met Chris's wife? Oh, Jesus! Your wife, man! Christ!

BARBARA: I've never met her.

JIM: Physically ... she's not bad.

BARBARA [*searching*]: Where's your tumblers?

JIM: Haven't got any. Total disorganization. Pat, I mean ... Runs about in her nightie till four in the afternoon. Waiting for Chris to come home from work and cook the dinner for the kids ...

CHRISTOPHER [*pointing to the cup on the table*]: We're not all going to drink from that one cup?

JIM: More in the cupboard ... Over there ...

[CHRISTOPHER *goes over to the cupboard.*]

BARBARA: Poor wee darling! After a hard day's work.

JIM: Up to his neck in shit.

CHRISTOPHER [*at cupboard*]: They're all cracked, for Christ's sake!

BARBARA [*giving him the one on the table*]: You can have this one, darling. It's whole.

CHRISTOPHER: What happens if I find out that frustration and unhappiness has been the main source of my creative energy? Give me that nail.

BARBARA [*giving him it*]: What are you going to do with it, darling?

CHRISTOPHER [*producing a bottle of Dettol from one of the cartons*]: Going to sterilize it.

JIM: Don't do that, you silly bugger! You'll spoil the alcohol.

CHRISTOPHER: You know what's going to happen here? I'm going to be too contented. Too happy ...

BARBARA: Hold it over the gas, if you must, darling ... Not Dettol, please!

CHRISTOPHER [*at the gas*]: See what I'm getting at? – What's the matter with your gas?

JIM: I think I can guarantee you'll be reasonably unhappy here. There's the climate, for a start . . .

CHRISTOPHER: What's happened to your gas?

JIM: There's no gas . . . Ran out six weeks ago . . . Use the fire for cooking . . . Cheaper . . .

BARBARA: What do you use? Peat?

JIM: Wood . . .

BARBARA: Oh . . . We must get some peat, tomorrow! Wouldn't that be gorgeous, darling . . . A real peat fire . . . And oil lamps . . .

CHRISTOPHER [*with the nail in his hand, searching for some way to sterilize it*]: I've got a point, haven't I. . . Supposing I need frustration for my artistic development . . . ?

BARBARA: Just give me that nail, darling . . . Nothing bad can come of a loving hand.

CHRISTOPHER: I'm asking you!

JIM: Supposing you need somebody to keep banging on your head with a five-pound hammer for your artistic development? Personally, fuck the artistic development – I'd rather do without the hammer.

CHRISTOPHER [*handing* BARBARA *the nail*]: This total disregard for hygiene, Jim! It's absolutely un-Marxist!

BARBARA [*mixing her potion*]: I've never found alcohol aphrodisiac – have you?

JIM: Beer, definitely, for me. Been drinking beer since I came up. Definite aphrodisiac. Three cans and I have to take to my shower!

BARBARA: This does give you a nice glow, mind . . .

JIM [*rummaging amongst the cartons*]: Any jam?

BARBARA: There's some jars of diabetic preserves somewhere . . . And two or three packets of slimming bread . .

JIM [*producing a carton of Durex*]: That should last you a wee while, anyway . . . And the dear ones!

BARBARA: Christopher and I have agreed that it would be criminal to bring children into a world poised on the brink of destruction.

CHRISTOPHER [*desperate*]: Look . . . I'll have to go to Ullapool . . . All sorts of essentials are needed. Tumblers . . .
tin-openers. . . . What about toilet paper? I bet you, you
haven't a scrap of toilet paper.

JIM: *Manchester Guardian*s and *Daily Worker*s. *Worker*s are
softer.

CHRISTOPHER: Newspapers can be very dangerous. Bac-
terial and abrasive.

JIM [*suddenly. On a new track*]: Christ! That's it! The Broadsheet! That's the real answer to Libberman. We'll expose
him! Annihilate the bugger!

   [CHRISTOPHER *making to go* . . .]

BARBARA: Darling! I've brought a whole carton of toilet
paper. Sit down.

JIM [*to* BARBARA]: Libberman brought out a broadsheet.
CALLING ALL WORKERS! May 1964. . . . For
May Day, you know?

BARBARA: What's Libberman like. . . . Christopher's always
talking about him. Is he nice? [*Handing* JIM *a drink.*]

JIM: He speaks nine languages.

CHRISTOPHER: To give you an idea, the kind of man he is:
he used his wife's maternity grant to pay for the broadsheets.

JIM [*to* BARBARA]: You'd like him. He's big, hairy and virile.
. . . Five kids. [*Drinking.*] This is great!

BARBARA: Les calls it 'Pink Jesus'.

JIM [*to* BARBARA]: A hundred thousand of the buggers, he
had printed. Attacking everybody on the Left – especially
us.

BARBARA: Actually; Les only thought up the name. A phar-
macist friend of ours gave us the recipe.

CHRISTOPHER [*desperate*]: Another thing. . . . My stomach
just will not stand unleavened bread – or cooking on a
fire. . . . I'm going to Ullapool. . . .

BARBARA: No, darling.

CHRISTOPHER: I'll only be an hour, dear. . . .

BARBARA: I said, 'no', darling. I don't want the party broken
up.

CHRISTOPHER: You know I don't like parties.... Neither do you.

JIM: Relax, man. Sit down.... [*To* BARBARA] Give him some more Red Jesus.

BARBARA: *Pink*. [*Making to pour him out some more.*]

CHRISTOPHER [*weakly*]: Please, Barbara ... I can't take too much alcohol. It gives me an acid stomach....

BARBARA [*putting her arms round him, protectively*]: Poor wee darling! You take a lot of looking after, don't you.... But you're going to get all you need from me. Aren't you, darling? Aren't you?

CHRISTOPHER [*with no great enthusiasm*]: Yes.

JIM: Libberman's wife's a real honey-pear! Fantastic! Small ... Very dark ... Always wears red. How we found out about this Broadsheet, was when I went up to his house, one night, to organize a united front on the Left, for spoiling the ballot papers, at the next election.

BARBARA: I don't see any point in that. Throwing away your vote!

CHRISTOPHER: You haven't got a vote. Not a real political choice.... Spoiling the ballot papers completely exposes British elections for what they really are – a giant confidence trick.

JIM [*continuing his story*]: The Broadsheets were stacked up all over the house. I was sorry for him. Him and his outfit had only been able to get rid of five thousand. I went into his lavatory.... He'd cut up the Broadsheets and hung them on a nail.... It was all right.... Soft enough....

BARBARA: Les hates anything but proper toilet paper.... If we ever ran out, he'd drive to the nearest Gents, about a mile away.... And come out with a roll under his jacket....

JIM: Long way to hold out.

BARBARA: Of course, he'd go long before he had to do anything.

JIM: Oh.

BARBARA: Stocking up. Just in case. He never made a row or anything about me not having it in.

JIM: Good boy!

BARBARA: Gorgeous, really. [*Going to the window.*]

JIM: Anything happen to him, that could happen to me?

BARBARA: Isn't it gorgeous here! I could be really happy in a place like this if it wasn't for the Nuclear Threat... Vietnam. . . .

JIM: Southern Rhodesia ... Malaysia ... Old Age Pensions ... Fluoridization of the Water Supply. . .

BARBARA: So many things to worry about, aren't there?

JIM: Safer here than Glasgow, mind. . . . Got a slight chance when it comes.

BARBARA: Have we?

JIM: We're not likely to get a direct hit. Gives us a bit more time. To adjust. . . . We can take poison or something. . . . more civilized. . . .

BARBARA: Have you got some poison?

JIM: Always dig up something. . . . Climb Stac Polly and jump off the top, maybe. . . . That should be a sure way out. . .

BARBARA: At sunset?

JIM: Any time you want. . . .

BARBARA [*to* CHRISTOPHER]: That should be the end of the novel, darling. . . . He climbs to the top of a mountain to drink in his last sight of the earth. . . . At sunset. . . . Everything is bathed in gold. The sea. . . . The lochs. . . . The islands. . . . In the distance, the big mushroom cloud is spreading . . . poisoning the beautiful earth. . . .

CHRISTOPHER: And the Scottish Symphony Orchestra playing *Götterdämmerung*.

BARBARA: Darling. . . . It's only a suggestion. . . .

CHRISTOPHER: Is my point about the British election system just not worth any comment? [JIM *looks at him, not knowing what he's talking about.*] I would've thought it was slightly more worthwhile discussing than purple suicides or the best substitutes for toilet paper.

BARBARA [*sharply*]: Darling. *You* introduced the subject of toilet paper!

JIM: And it's those ordinary, common objects and functions that are the root of all political action. . . . Toilet paper leads to a new critique of Libberman and with the annihilation of Libberman the uniting of our two parties ... and on and on and on. .... Christ! That's a real insight! Isn't that an insight, boy?

BARBARA: It's absolutely true, Jim!

JIM: It's a real insight. You know you're the first woman I've met, who's sparked off insights in me. It's usually the other way round. They damp them out in a blanket of sensuality.

BARBARA [*flattered*]: Did I spark that off?

JIM: I'm telling you! You keep doing it. I've had dozens of minor insights all the time we've been talking.

CHRISTOPHER: I can see now! It was a disastrous mistake! We should never have come here!

BARBARA [*to* CHRISTOPHER]: Darling. ... What you said about British elections. ... It was just ... so right. ... It didn't call for any further comment. ...

CHRISTOPHER: I can see exactly how the situation is going to develop. It was an absolutely selfish action to come here. ... A betrayal of Marxism.

BARBARA: Darling. ... Just because Jim and I were discussing –

CHRISTOPHER [*to* BARBARA]: Jim has one of the major tasks of the century in front of him. ... His twentieth-century re-statement of Marxism is desperately needed. He can't afford to get emotionally involved with you or any other woman. ... He's wasted enough of his life on that kind of thing. ...

JIM: Christ! Yes! All those wasted years. ... When I could have been thinking, having insights ... writing. ...

CHRISTOPHER [*with a kind of paternal, indulgent rebuke*]: Yes, Jim. Your best years.

JIM: And all I did was get involved with women. [*To* BARBARA] I've got this bloody habit... Of getting involved with women... Even pros... I used to pick up a pro. ...

BARBARA: Often?

JIM: Now and then. ... And I hadn't –

BARBARA [*to* CHRISTOPHER]: Did you, darling?

CHRISTOPHER [*conveying the impression of limitless sexual experience*]: Well. ...

BARBARA: I understand, darling. . . . Everybody has different intensities of sexual drives and have –

JIM: Christopher doesn't believe in it. It's un-Marxist – Prostitution. . . . And he never has any spare cash, anyway. . . . But when I pick one up . . . I haven't got in her bed . . . when I start getting involved . . . and emotional bonds start creeping up between us. . . . I keep bloody missing them for weeks afterwards! I start believing that I can't live without them! It's fantastic!

BARBARA: I think it'll be three or four generations of socialism, before we eradicate Prostitution. . . .

JIM: It finishes me for weeks! I mean. . . My wife. . . It took me months to get over that. . . .

BARBARA: What happened to her?

JIM: She ran away with her husband. Catholic. . . . She couldn't get a divorce.

CHRISTOPHER: I'm sorry, Jim. . . . I didn't think out my actions to their logical conclusion. . . . It was absolutely selfish of me, coming up here with Barbara. . . .

JIM: Relax, boy. If I get involved – I get involved. . . .

BARBARA: I'm certainly not moving from here, tonight, darling. . . . I've done quite enough travelling for one day. And Jim *wants* me to stay . . . don't you, Jim.

JIM: Christ, yes! I'm telling you! You spark off insights in me!

CHRISTOPHER: Jim doesn't know what he wants. He has to be protected against himself. . . . Look at all those years he –

JIM: What are you planning to do, then, boy? Take her back to Les?

BARBARA: That would be sheer cruelty. . . . Just when he's getting nicely settled in with his mother. . . .

JIM: What the hell's he doing with his mother?

CHRISTOPHER: He's impotent. Her husband is impotent.

BARBARA: It's nothing psychological. . . . He had lung trouble. . . . Two years after our marriage. . . .

JIM: What did you do when he went that way?

CHRISTOPHER: It was nothing to do with his lungs. . . .

BARBARA: Of course it was! It's a very common effect of lung trouble.

CHRISTOPHER: It's a social symptom.... The result of the false relationship of the individual to his environment in Capitalist society....

BARBARA: Sometimes, darling, you come out with some absolute shit!

CHRISTOPHER [*continuing his analysis*]: Sucked dry by conformity, drained of all inner resources....

BARBARA: Les happens to be, darling, a natural born Socialist....

CHRISTOPHER [*knocked off his dialectical balance*]: Oh.... You never told me he was a Socialist....

BARBARA: Did I need to, darling? Did you imagine I could have sexual relations with a politically unconscious man? I couldn't.... They repel me ... physically and spiritually....

JIM: What did you do when he went that way?

BARBARA: I struggled with myself.

JIM: That was nice.

BARBARA: I don't believe in promiscuity.... I believe in love and sex – not one without the other....

JIM: It must have been murder for poor Les.

BARBARA: Why should it have been? He knew I understood. ... We discussed the problem openly... It brought us even closer together....

JIM: How long have you held out? I'm interested, because it might have some bearing on the future length of my endurance – Maybe, I could be encouraged by your example.

BARBARA: Seven years.

JIM [*visibly impressed*]: Seven years! Jesus! I couldn't begin to compete with seven years! Christ! Seven years!

BARBARA: And don't think I'm frigid or under-sexed!

JIM: I should think such a thing, honey-pear!

BARBARA: Neither was Les.

CHRISTOPHER: Nor is Pat. As far as her sexuality is –

BARBARA: Till it happened, we had a fabulous time! Les is a traveller and works a five-day week.... We'd stay in bed all Saturday morning.... And sometimes go back in the afternoon.... After lunch.... It was wonderful....

JIM [*drinking her in, amorously*]: Christ, honey! It must have been!

BARBARA: I just wasn't interested in any other men. Never. ... Even after it happened.... Till Christopher.... [*Giving him a loving look.*]

CHRISTOPHER [*rebuking her*]: Till *Prague*, Barbara....

JIM: Prague?

CHRISTOPHER: Progressive Tours....

BARBARA: He was gorgeous! I could have loved him – even more than Les *or* Christopher – A Captain in the Soviet Air Force....

JIM: Ivan?

BARBARA: Boris.... He was big.... Massive.... Like a cliff against me.... Lovely cropped hair ... with little attractive silver grey flecks here and there.... I love cropped hair in a man! And beautiful golden skin. [CHRISTOPHER *winces.*] He was beautiful.... You should've seen him in swimming trunks! I could've eaten him up....

CHRISTOPHER [*rummaging in the case*]: I think I'd better have a Disprin....

BARBARA: Oh.... My poor wee pet.... Is your head very bad....

CHRISTOPHER [*responding to the maternal treatment*]: A little bit, dear....

BARBARA: You just sit down there.... And I'll get them for you.... [*Feeling his brow.*] It's a bit hot.... [*As she is going about organizing the Disprins....*] He was in his mid-forties. ... At nights, I cried to think of a man like that wasted on a nonentity of a wife! He actually carried her photograph in his wallet! Straight hair.... No dress sense.... Sexless... Like a reactionary press photograph of the typical Russian woman! [*Handing* CHRISTOPHER *the Disprins and a cup of water.*] There you are, darling.... Just take that ... and you'll soon be better....

CHRISTOPHER [*about to drink when he checks himself*]: Where does your water come from, Jim?

BARBARA [*to* JIM]: We were staying at the same hotel. Just drawn to each other.... Magnetic....

CHRISTOPHER: Jim.... Where does your water come from?

JIM: I don't know.... Never thought about it.... Sometimes it has a mild taste of cow-shit.... But most of the time it's all right.

CHRISTOPHER: I believe, Jim, that you're either a Marxist ... or not a Marxist....

BARBARA: The climax came on the last night of the holiday. ... We'd been having dinner –

JIM [*to* BARBARA]: I thought you hadn't –

CHRISTOPHER: If you're a Marxist – it should enter into every facet of your life.

BARBARA: Feelings were running very high between us.... You can imagine.... Our last dinner.... And it was very hot in the restaurant....

CHRISTOPHER: Your attitude to the water-supply.... Water purity is very important....

BARBARA [*trying to shut him up*]: Darling.... It looks crystal clean....

CHRISTOPHER: Prince Albert died of typhus, drinking water in Buckingham Palace....

BARBARA: This isn't Buckingham Palace, darling....

CHRISTOPHER: You see the dialectical situation.... One of the pillars of the system destroyed by one of the diseases the system created....

JIM: You were having dinner....

BARBARA: I was wearing a nylon dress.... Nylon can be very hot.... He noticed.... 'Are you feeling tired?' He had a fabulous, rich Russian accent.... I could just sit, with my eyes closed, listening to him.... 'Perhaps you would like to change into something cooler....' He was always so thoughtful and considerate....

CHRISTOPHER: Well, you can be, for a week together.... That's hardly the test, is it.... A week together in an hotel!

BARBARA: No.... But I'm sure, darling.... That's what he'd've been like for life! He was that type of man....

CHRISTOPHER [*putting down the cup*]: I'll take them with some Pink Jesus.

BARBARA: 'Well, Boris,' I said, 'I think I will change into a linen dress'....

CHRISTOPHER [*hesitating with his cup of Pink Jesus*]: I'm wondering if alcohol mightn't react dangerously with the Disprin.

JIM [*hanging on to* BARBARA's *story*]: No.... It's great, Chris.... They work together....

BARBARA: 'I will escort you up to your room,' he said. Standing up, like the perfect gentleman he was.... You've never seen such manners!

CHRISTOPHER [*at last taking the Disprins*]: I suppose it'll be all right.

BARBARA: You can imagine how the tension was rising. I was absolutely *sure* something was going to happen, now. ... He took my arm –

JIM [*something suddenly occurring to him*]: Barbara, honey.... Just out of curiosity.... What would have been your reaction to Boris if ... say ... he had had some ... kind of minor blemish....

BARBARA [*puzzled*]: Blemish?

JIM: Yes.... Only temporary.... Nothing infectious.... A skin blemish....

BARBARA: He was perfect.... Absolutely beautiful....

JIM: Yes.... But if he had a rash. Ugly ... and nasty.... [CHRISTOPHER *has a coughing fit over his cup.*]

BARBARA: Darling! What's happened?

CHRISTOPHER: Disprin and alcohol.... Burning my stomach....

BARBARA: Poor wee pet! [*Stroking his hair.*]

JIM: What would've been your reaction?

BARBARA: Reaction?

JIM: To Boris with a blotchy skin.

BARBARA: I was absolutely positive we were going to have intercourse. You understand ... I loved him. We went into my room.... But he turned his back on me while I slipped off my dress. I was standing there in my bra and panties....

JIM: Black?

BARBARA: White, actually....

JIM: Just a point of information. . . .

BARBARA: My whole body was drawn to him. . . . Like a magnet. . . . I had to keep myself from going to him. . . .

JIM: And still he kept his back turned.

BARBARA: I even went in front of him, pretending I was looking for something. He turned his head away. There was nothing else I could do. I just slipped on another dress. . . . Did up my hair and face. . . . And we went downstairs. . . .

We had breakfast together, the next morning. . . . Then we shook hands . . . and he flew back to Russia. . . .

But just imagine! What self-control he must have had. I was standing there. . . . He must have heard my breathing. . . . In my bra and panties. . . . He must have known I was waiting for him. . . . And he didn't look. . . . Not till I had done up my last button. . . .

JIM: A masochist *voyeur*.

CHRISTOPHER: Maybe he had lung trouble, Barbara. . . . Like your Les. . . .

BARBARA: He had three kids, darling. . . .

CHRISTOPHER: Since the kids, Barbara.

JIM: Definitely some kind of exotic perversion. . . . Very interesting.

BARBARA: You see! Neither of you understand. . . . And it's so obvious. . . .

JIM: To come back to that skin blemish. . . .

BARBARA: He hadn't any blemish. . . . I told you. . . . He had a beautiful, golden skin.

JIM: But if he had?

BARBARA: It's so obvious what was going on in his mind. . . . He was a real Socialist. . . . In mind *and* body. He wanted me as much as I wanted him. But he . . . he . . . You know what I'm trying to say. . . .

JIM: Subjected the situation to Marxist analysis . . . ?

BARBARA: Yes. . . . That's exactly what he did! He had a wife, and children, and an important part to play in building World Socialism.

CHRISTOPHER: Just as a point of information, Barbara, New Socialists do *not* accept Soviet society as Socialist. . . .

JIM: No.... But evolving towards it....

CHRISTOPHER: Oh, yes.... Moving to Socialism.... That's obvious. Only dilettantes like Libberman and his crowd see the Soviet as moving –

JIM: About this skin blemish [*she is about to protest again*] – I mean ... if he had a blemish....

BARBARA: I told you. I was ready to love Boris.... In every sense of the word. You love in spite of – not because of. That means –

JIM: So even if Boris had been covered with a nasty, flaming red rash from tip to toe – temporarily, of course ... you –

BARBARA: I happen to be a very mature person. When I love – I love. But Boris had a beautiful skin. Perfect....

JIM: But even if he hadn't, it would have made no difference to you?

BARBARA: Of course it wouldn't!

JIM: There you are, boy! You're worrying over nothing. I knew it. Barbara is a very mature person.

BARBARA: I am. Very.

CHRISTOPHER: All Socialists are.... Real Socialists.

JIM: Barbara.... Christopher has ... well ... not what you and I would consider a problem – but something that has been weighing heavily on his mind.

CHRISTOPHER: I'd rather we didn't discuss it.

BARBARA: Darling! We don't need to hide our problems from each other! I'm very angry with you, darling!

CHRISTOPHER: You can't help, here, dear.... Honestly....

BARBARA: Now.... Come on.... What's worrying you, pet? [*Takes his hand.*]

JIM: Not Boris, Barbara – but Christopher – has this flaming, red rash –

CHRISTOPHER: Look Jim, this is something between Barbara and –

JIM: From tip to toe.... All over his body.... But temporary. ... Absolutely temporary.... Show her! [*He goes over to open* CHRISTOPHER's *shirt....* CHRISTOPHER *retreats.*]

BARBARA: Darling! You're not really worried about a little thing like that! Are you? Really now! [CHRISTOPHER *begins to see some hope. And at the same time with the hope more despair. But for the moment hope is dominant. He unbends a little, takes his hands away from his chest. . . .*] You're just like a big baby. [*Suddenly . . . it occurring to her . . . and involuntarily backing away from him*] It isn't infectious, is it, darling?

CHRISTOPHER: Of course it's not infectious. It's an allergy.

BARBARA: The salmon we had at Spean Bridge?

CHRISTOPHER: It's a very nasty, ugly red rash. Just as if I'd been bitten by horseflies all over my body. Lumpy, too. . . . [BARBARA *tries to hide her revulsion at the description.*]

JIM: Do you not listen to people, man? Barbara's just told you. You've got a totally wrong attitude to this. Lovers are not repelled by each other's rashes.

[CHRISTOPHER *looks questioningly at* BARBARA.]

BARBARA: You're *sure* it's not infectious, darling. . . . Just in case you might need medical attention. . . .

CHRISTOPHER: It is not infectious.

BARBARA: And it'll go away. . . . It won't last for ever?

CHRISTOPHER: It'll go away.

BARBARA: What are you worried about then, darling?

CHRISTOPHER: Because, Barbara, it will go away – when I go away.

BARBARA: I don't understand you, darling. . . .

CHRISTOPHER: When I go away – from you.

JIM: That's a totally wrong analysis! This is the major challenge of your life. That rash is a kind of moral appendicitis.

CHRISTOPHER: Jim, I know my own body! For Christ's sake!

JIM: A vestige of a past, diseased society that was rooted in total subservience to an arbitrary ethical code. . . . The Ten Commandments. . . .

CHRISTOPHER: I'm against the Ten Commandments.

JIM: Try to build a motor-car engine on the principle that gases expand when they're cooled.

BARBARA: Do they?

CHRISTOPHER: The Law of Thermodynamics, Barbara. They contract.

JIM: You won't go anywhere with that car. Are you going to

capitulate to the totally irrational code of a dying society? You just going to run away from the challenge, like you've been doing all your life? It's so simple, man! All you've got to do is take it up.... And your skin'll turn clean overnight.

CHRISTOPHER [*thinking*]: I admit it's moral weakness, running away.... Yes.... I can see that, now.

BARBARA: Of course it is, darling!

CHRISTOPHER: But.... Are you sure, Barbara, *you* can....

BARBARA: Darling! I'm very angry with you! To even *think* a little thing like a rash would make the slightest difference to our relationship.

JIM: We're Socialists, man. New Socialists! Nothing under the sun is alien to man. Fear is the distorting mirror of life. Yes. It's been said before, boy.... But we mean it and live it!

BARBARA [*kissing* CHRISTOPHER]: Silly boy! Getting yourself all worked up over a wee thing like that!

JIM: If it had been the other way round, and Barbara had had the rash...

BARBARA: I must say ... I've never had any of that kind of trouble. I've always had a clear, healthy –

JIM: No. But if you had, honey ... Christopher wouldn't have been repelled.

CHRISTOPHER: I'd've loved her all the more.

JIM: No. No. Just the same. All the more's running into perversion.

CHRISTOPHER: True.... True, Jim.

JIM: You would've loved her just the same. That's it, isn't it, boy?

CHRISTOPHER: That's the Socialist way.

JIM: Absolutely.

CHRISTOPHER: And you're sure.... It doesn't make any difference between us?

BARBARA: Darling! I really am getting angry with you!

CHRISTOPHER [*taking her hand*]: You're a marvellous girl, Barbara! Wonderful! God! I'd lost faith people like you existed! Pat wouldn't have been able to *look* at me, like this.

BARBARA: Pat.

JIM: Ten-Commandment-ridden Pat!

CHRISTOPHER: I'd've had to sleep on a couch. Anything like that ... disgusts her ... even with the children.... I just can't get over the way you're taking it.... It's ...

BARBARA: That's the way I'm made, darling! A thing like that doesn't bother me.

CHRISTOPHER [*with growing confidence, or pulled by a drive at another level*]: It *is* very nasty, dear. Look. See for yourself. [*He opens his shirt.* BARBARA *steels herself to take the shock but the reality is rather more than she bargained for. She just manages to hide her revulsion.*]

BARBARA [*backing slightly away*]: Poor darling! Is it all over?

CHRISTOPHER [*almost boasting. Flaunting it*]: From tip to toe. I'll show you my leg – [*making to lift his trouser leg.*]

BARBARA: It's all right, darling ... I've seen it.

CHRISTOPHER: And you don't mind it ... I can see. You're wonderful, dear! Like my mother.... My mother, when I was a kid. Once, when I was sick in bed.... She wiped it up.... With love....

BARBARA [*trying to get out*]: A few days in the open air, darling.... With lots of sun.... And you'll be fine. We'll give you loads of greens ... and salads and things....

JIM: You don't need to. The first time you sleep together – he'll be cured. [*She stiffens at this.*] Wake up fresh and pink like a water baby.

BARBARA: We'll get lots of apples for you. Apples are wonderful for the skin!

JIM: You don't need apples. I'm telling you. The sure way to get rid of that rash –

BARBARA [*sharply*]: Jim ... I appreciate you having us here. But would you please let us work out our own problems.

JIM: You can't.... Obviously you're incapable....

BARBARA: But you are!

CHRISTOPHER: He has made some valuable comments, Barbara....

JIM: I'm just saving you wasting time on useless discussion. ... You don't need to worry about diet ... or fresh air ...

or ointments ... or anything. Once you and Christopher – get into bed together....

CHRISTOPHER: He's right, Barbara. I'm sure he's right.

BARBARA [*groping for a way out*]: Darling ... I don't see that ... I don't see that, at all....

CHRISTOPHER: You don't see it?

BARBARA: You see, darling.... It would've been entirely different if we had had intercourse before....

JIM: Of course it would. He wouldn't have had a rash.

BARBARA [*ignoring him*]: But our first time, darling.... I've been looking forward to this, for so long....

CHRISTOPHER: So have I, Barbara....

BARBARA: It's so important, darling, that our first time, should be ... unspoiled ... beautiful.... Perfect, darling ...

CHRISTOPHER: Yes. I see that, Barbara....

JIM: This is an imperfect world. If you want to survive, you have to be continually compromising between the ideal and reality.

BARBARA: You've got to appreciate my sexual background, darling. It's been so long....

JIM: Christ, yes! Seven years!

BARBARA: The first time is going to be very important to me.... This way ... it could easily throw a shadow over our whole life together.

CHRISTOPHER: I don't see that. I don't follow your reasoning, Barbara.

JIM: Sheer metaphysics! The cult of Virginity. The exaggeration of the significance of the first penetration. Another vestige of the property society....

BARBARA [*getting ratty*]: I don't care what it is. That's how I feel! [*To* CHRISTOPHER] Darling, you wouldn't feel right either, now.... Would you?

CHRISTOPHER: I'd be all right ... if you were.

BARBARA: Just think, darling.... Just try and imagine it.... I would be conscious of you being uncertain ... unsure. ... You would be imagining me, turning away from your body....

CHRISTOPHER: I wouldn't.

BARBARA: You would, darling ... I'm sure.... Your self-confidence would be shaken....

CHRISTOPHER: Don't worry about that, Barbara ... I'd be fine ... I've never had any kind of impotence complex.

BARBARA: Darling, just use your imagination! It's obvious! I know.... You would be conscious all the time of that ugly rash.

[CHRISTOPHER *turns and holds on to the admission 'ugly rash', realizes now he's fighting a losing battle. She is no longer accessible, consequently he is no longer interested in her.*]

CHRISTOPHER: Oh. You do find it ugly. You admit it, now!

JIM: Christ, Christopher! There's no argument about it. It's bloody revolting, man!

CHRISTOPHER [*to* BARBARA. *An interrogation*]: My body repels you. Does it?

BARBARA: Darling, you –

CHRISTOPHER: Does it?

BARBARA: Darling, I've explained –

CHRISTOPHER: It's a simple question. Does it or does it not repel you?

BARBARA: Darling. It hardly *attracts* me! Don't be ridiculous!

CHRISTOPHER: Right. That's established. My body repels you. Consequently, you find it impossible to sleep with me.

BARBARA: That does not mean I don't love you.

CHRISTOPHER: Do you or do you not find it impossible to sleep with me?

BARBARA: I'm disappointed in you, Christopher. I'm sorry ... I expected more understanding from *you* ...

JIM [*shifting sides, and clearing the way for making a bid himself for* BARBARA]: Put it this way, Comrade. If food is served up, visually repulsive, it takes away your appetite.

CHRISTOPHER [*studying* BARBARA]: I can see now. I have the objective picture. It's gelling at last.... You don't want a sexual partner – You want an instrument.... A mutual masturbation society!

JIM: You could counter my analogy by pointing out that if you're really hungry ... you'll eat up any mess.... But that's lust – not love.... That doesn't invalidate the analogy.

CHRISTOPHER: You bloody intellectuals! Social Justice Fanatics! Pink Jesuses!

BARBARA: I cannot go to bed and make love with a man whose body is covered with ugly, raised, repulsive, scarlet blotches ... I'm sorry....

CHRISTOPHER: With your *Manchester Guardians* ... and *New Statesmen*! Don't think I'm worried about not sleeping with you! I couldn't care less about that now ... It's the bloody hypocrisy ... The Christian Tolerance ... The Angelic humanism ... Nothing under the sun is alien to us! This bloody eternal posing....

BARBARA: It was not posing. I am not in the habit of –

CHRISTOPHER: Your whole performance was posing ... and don't try to argue about it!

JIM: Wait, boy.... This is a new situation. Obviously, your rash worries Barbara. In that case, if you slept with her ...

CHRISTOPHER: When I want to be psychoanalysed, Jim, I'll go to an analyst!

JIM: Her tensions will be communicated to you. You understand.... Your rash could even go worse....

CHRISTOPHER [*getting his cases together*]: You know ... When I look at you ... I'm sorry for you....

BARBARA: Christopher, much as I love you, I know it would be a disastrous –

CHRISTOPHER: Christ! I am. I'm sorry for you.... You're the real tragic figures.... Not the semi-detached, collar-and-tie robots you're always sneering at. Yours is the real tragedy! Sneering at their Sunday morning car washing, their telly-glazed eyes, their life-insulated existence....

BARBARA [*stung*]: Oh, you admire that kind of life, do you? You think that's what we should all do. Capitulate to conformity and join the other vegetables....

CHRISTOPHER: Listen to the automatic responses! Programmed for the cause. Feed in the appropriate card – and out comes the printed answer.

BARBARA: Go on, then. Get back to your semi-detached cemetery. And your beautiful relationship with Pat – who doesn't even care enough about you to sew a button on your bloody shirt! And your important, creative work on the *Clydesdale Courant* — writing lists of the mourners at the latest Tory funeral and articles on Territorial manoeuvres. ... Don't let me stop you from fulfilling yourself!

JIM: No! This is sheer violence we're moving into! If we're going to master this problem, we have to get closer to each other. For Christ's sake don't put up the barriers of violence!

CHRISTOPHER: I'm not ashamed of my *Courant* job! If that's selling your soul — All right ... I've sold it. Did any of you Socialists offer to pull me out of the bloody buses? Getting up at five in the morning.... Walking through the dark to the Depot.... Low.... Right at the bottom.... It was a dirty capitalist who pulled me out of that shit. And I'm grateful to him. I'm bloody grateful to him. He's done a damn sight more for me than you bloody Socialists!

BARBARA: If I had any idea that you were so immature and selfish ...

CHRISTOPHER: Look what I am now ... I'm somebody in the town. People know me, M.P.s and businessmen stand me drinks, chase after me to write them up. I've pulled myself out of the shit. What's stopping the other proles from doing the same? If they want to stay there, let them! I hate them! I hate them! They frighten me! Rang-gers! Rang-gers — Rang-gers ... This-tle This-tle. This-tle.... Their blank, bloody faces.... Chanting away ... Ran-Gers! Ran-Gers! Ran-Gers! Why the hell should I fight for those bastards? Eh, I'm asking you?

JIM: Boy, if you don't want to fight, don't; why should you?

CHRISTOPHER: All right, tell me, give me some reason.... What's the point? Three, four generations ... of us ... fighting for Socialism.... Where has it got us?

BARBARA: It's got two thirds of the world somewhere — hasn't it?

CHRISTOPHER [*ignoring her*]: Where has it got us?... You see, you can't answer. You don't want to answer. Nowhere ... that's where it's got us.... Am I right?

JIM: Christ! How the fuckin' hell do I know, man! To me,

it's like water on a stone. . . . It takes centuries before it cuts through – but it cuts through in the end. . . .

CHRISTOPHER: Yes. Well, let my great, great grandchildren look after their bloody selves! I've got *my* life to live. That's the only real honest programme. [*An insight.*] That's what I want! Honesty! If you hate the blacks – for Christ's sake don't walk about with Anti-Racialist banners. If homos repel you – don't bloody petition Parliament for Homo Reform – If you don't like mixing with Jews –

JIM: Oh. Honesty! That's your programme, eh?

CHRISTOPHER: For Christ's sake! What else is there?

JIM: What honesty, like, boy? Like *honest* fucking Nazis sending the Jews up the chimneys of Buchenwald? Or *honest*, all-American boys kicking in the balls of fucking niggers! Like *honest* perverts screwing little girls in *honest* lust. That honesty?

CHRISTOPHER [*shaken*]: Christ! I don't mean that . . . I don't mean that, Jim!

JIM: What do you mean then, Christopher?

CHRISTOPHER: I don't know. . . . The whole world's a bloody balls-up!

JIM: What do you want, Christopher? What do you want?

BARBARA: I'm certainly not going back to Glasgow with you. At least I was honest enough to cut all my connexions there. *I've* given in my notice . . . and I've written to Les. . . .

CHRISTOPHER [*ignores her. He is completely immersed in* JIM'S *question*]: What do I want?

JIM [*to* BARBARA]: You're staying here, honey-pear. Everything's organized for you. . . . Peat fires, paraffin lights, bog myrtle. . . .

BARBARA [*as a kind of last attempt for* CHRISTOPHER]: Make up your mind, Christopher. What are you going to do?

JIM: He's going home to Glasgow.

CHRISTOPHER: That's the key question! What do I want?

BARBARA: I've got my dressing-gown in your case. I'd better get it out.

[*She goes over to the cases, finally abandoning all hope of having* CHRISTOPHER. *From this point she moves closer to* JIM, *looking at him from time to time and gradually becoming so attracted to him she hardly sees* CHRISTOPHER.]

CHRISTOPHER [*looking round the posters*]: Is that what I want? No war in Vietnam. Feed the Starving Asians. Yanks get out of Holy Loch.

BARBARA: What's wrong with that? If everybody who really wanted all those things joined together and –

CHRISTOPHER: Is that what I want? *Tribune* ... The *Worker* ... The *New Statesman* ... tells me that's what I *should* want. But do I? I've got such a load of righteous, honourable, correct desires loaded on top of me.... All that lumber piled up.... Where the hell am I, under it all?

BARBARA: It's emotionally immature, unstable people like you who discredit the whole movement! Isn't that right, Jim?

JIM: If you want to make Glasgow tonight, boy ...

CHRISTOPHER: What have I been aiming at? What have I been trying to do with my life?

BARBARA: He'd probably be better to stop somewhere half-way, and spend the night there....

CHRISTOPHER [*another inspiration*]: You know what it's like. ... It's like bowls! You know ... The bowls they play in the parks. They're biased. You see? The one way you can be sure of never hitting the jack is to aim directly for it.

JIM: Good insight that. Seminal. Yes. Worth working on, that....

CHRISTOPHER [*racing to grab this new key to the universe*]: You understand? We aim our lives in the direction of the jack. ... But the bias pulls us further and further away from it.... Barbara ... I'm sorry ... It's my fault ... I'm entirely responsible. Without really thinking it out, I pressed you into coming with me ... and breaking with Les ... I'm sorry, Barbara ... I'm sorry....

BARBARA: All right. Don't beat your breast about it. Do you remember what I did with my raincoat? I can't see it among my things.

CHRISTOPHER: It's in my big case ... there. [*Giving it to her.*]

JIM: Christopher, I don't want to rush you ...

CHRISTOPHER: Yes ... I'm going ... I don't think it's been a wasted journey.

JIM [*looking at* BARBARA, *who returns the look*]: Christ! No, Christopher! By no means!

CHRISTOPHER: We've uncovered new insights.... Moved nearer the objective truth....

JIM: Yes ... Definitely.

CHRISTOPHER: I'll do some more thinking on this ... Send you something on it for the next issue.

JIM [*pushing him out*]: Great, boy ... Fine.

CHRISTOPHER: We've got to retrace our steps ... Go back to the beginning ... On this new basis ...

JIM: We have, yes, you're right, Christopher.
[*They make to see him out.*]

CHRISTOPHER: Don't come out. It's too wet.
[*They stand at the door, watching him, and wave as he drives off, then move over to the table.*]

JIM [*pours out a Pink Jesus for* BARBARA *and himself*]: That's Christopher happy again. Isn't that nice. Making your friends happy.

BARBARA: Did *we* do it?

JIM: He'll be singing his Gems from Gilbert and Sullivan all the way home!

BARBARA: And Les is happy, too.

JIM: Yes, Les is happy, too.

BARBARA: Sometimes an Oedipus complex can be very useful, can't it?

JIM: I still can't get over that seven years, honey-pear! Jesus! That's some time to store up an orgasm.

BARBARA: Oh ... that ...

JIM: Big responsibility ... A seven year orgasm!

BARBARA: That was just for Christopher ... You know what he's like. He's one of those people you couldn't ever be absolutely honest with, could you? [JIM *waits for the confession.*] There were odd times ... now and then ... A very intelligent book traveller ... Used to come to Glasgow every two or three months ... And a gorgeous teacher in the Committee of a Hundred ... But not all that often. At odd times ... I mean, darling ... Could you blame me?

JIM [*taking her hands*]: Honey-pear! You're beautiful! Fantastic!

BARBARA: It's absolutely true about Boris. Every word!

JIM: Honey-pear, go'n change into something warmer. It's getting cold.

BARBARA: I think I will. It is getting coldish. I've got a gorgeous, knitted dress.... Red, dark red.... Do you like dark red?

JIM: Beautiful. You can change in the bedroom there....

[*They go towards the bedroom. He helps her with her cases.*]

[JIM *comes out again, thinking. He stands, torn by the two forces, the conflict that has dominated his life ... sex and freedom ... on the brink.*

The sun comes up. He goes to the window and looks out, then back to the bedroom where BARBARA *can be heard, humming 'The Lark in the Clear Air'. Somewhere from the Loch shore a curlew cries. He takes a rucksack from the corner and looks at it ... then throws it down again – the combination of apathy and desire for* BARBARA *being too much for him.*

He takes up his editorial, puts it into the machine and begins to type rapidly ... waiting for some sign from BARBARA.]

BARBARA [*from the bedroom door*]: Jim! Jim!

JIM: Yes, sweetheart?

BARBARA: Could you bring in my handbag, darling, please. ... It's on the table.

JIM: Sure ... Sure ... [*He rises, unpins a couple of peace movement badges from his dressing-gown, re-pins them on his shoulders, like officers' pips. He takes a cap from the floor and places it on his head, Guards style.*]

BARBARA [*impatiently*]: Can't you find it, darling?

JIM: Coming, honey-pear! Coming ... [*Takes a deep breath, straightens up, places the bag under his arm, and marches into the bedroom, like a perfect moral Communist, humming the Soviet national anthem.*]

CURTAIN

GEORGE MULLY

The Master of Two Servants

AN ANALYTIC FARCE

The Master of Two Servants was first performed at the Traverse Theatre in March 1965, with the following cast:

HERBERT	Noel Collins
ROSEMARY	Kate Coleridge
CHIQUITA	Frances Davison
OMAR	Charles Baptiste

Directed by GEORGE MULLY

Herbert and Rosemary's house. The dining-room. HERBERT *and*
ROSEMARY *are seated at either end of the table.*

*They are a bored couple. They wear dressing-gowns and are going
through a large pile of newspapers. Several empty coffee cups suggest
they have been occupied this way for a considerable time and at the
expense of everything else.*

*The table itself is a behemoth, a wall-to-wall table filling the entire
room. As it occupies so much space,* HERBERT *and* ROSEMARY
*occasionally have to mount it or crawl under it. They regard it as a
benign growth to which they have been long accustomed.*

*There is a sideboard in the room and three doors lead to the kitchen,
the bedrooms and an outside hall.*

*During a short overture they read listlessly to themselves a moment
and then rapidly aloud. Music is heard between verses as they turn the
pages of their newspapers. (Background music should be used exten-
sively throughout the play.)*

HERBERT:	What outrageous defiance
ROSEMARY:	The marvels of science
BOTH:	Unbelievable, what's going on.
HERBERT:	The Sultan is better
ROSEMARY:	They've found that lost letter
BOTH:	They're building a dam on the Don.
ROSEMARY:	What incredible daring
HERBERT:	What does *she* think she's wearing?
BOTH:	There are some things one cannot forgive
ROSEMARY:	New hope for arthritics.
HERBERT:	He's sueing the critics.
BOTH:	It's indecent how some people live.

[*Rosemary takes off her glasses.*]

ROSEMARY:	May I interrupt you for a second, dear . . .?
HERBERT:	There's a most curious article here.
ROSEMARY:	There is something I think you should know

HERBERT: Eh? Oh, certainly, love, quite so.

ROSEMARY: Something about the house, you see
HERBERT: Whatever it is, dear, I'm sure I'll agree
ROSEMARY: Since we've broadened our interest in life
             I'm a much less effective wife
HERBERT: Come now, my dear,
ROSEMARY: It's true
             I've rather neglected you.

> From Monday to Friday
> The house is untidy
> On weekends the Sundays intrude
> I've given up cooking
> In favour of looking
> Through columns devoted to food
>
> I don't mind admitting
> That all of this sitting
> And reading and mental massage
> Has never conceded
> The time that is needed
> To manage a happy ménage
>
> With life so beguiling
> The laundry is piling
> The knives coated with marmalade
> Domestic redressing
> Continued so pressing
> That I've had to hire a maid!
>
> Logic had to be obeyed
> I hired a maid.

HERBERT: But darling, how sensible
            [*He sits, delighted, on the table.*]
ROSEMARY: You think it's defensible?
HERBERT: Thoroughly
ROSEMARY: Good
        I hoped you would.
        She's coming on the morning train ...

HERBERT: This morning?

ROSEMARY: And we must explain
Her duties to her. Should we dress?

HERBERT: I suppose we should, but first, I must confess
That due to my laxity about the house ...

ROSEMARY: I rather think a skirt and blouse
Would be all right

HERBERT: Yes, quite so
But let me finish before you go

As you've noticed the garden needs some attention ...

ROSEMARY: It's thoroughly covered with weeds
... And cries for intervention

HERBERT: So I've hired a gardener to see to its needs.

A gardener
Will pacify the earth with tender care
Will charm the buds to grow and scent the
    air
Will regiment the colours with design
And fashion arabesques of shapely vine

A gardener
Will nourish striving blooms with knowing
    hands
Until each one in open glory stands,
Upright, robust and firm they hold aloof
Against all man-made beauty stern reproof

All this and more
A gardener brings.
Love, from his lore,
Serenely springs.

ROSEMARY: A gardener, our own gardener, how thrilling
[*She is quite pleased.*]

HERBERT: New growth, so rewarding

ROSEMARY: fulfilling

[*They return gradually to their newspapers.*]

ROSEMARY: Oh, darling, that was a smart move
I can't tell you how much I approve
With the house in such capable hands
We can manage its many demands
Enrich ourselves and thrive at little cost.

HERBERT: I'm delighted to hear you approve
We've *each* made a rather good move
It's not comfort but time that we seek
For the Sundays grow larger each week
And a day without the dailies and we're lost.

BOTH: Now kitchen and garden
Will grant us a pardon
ROSEMARY: From Brillo
HERBERT: and stern daffodil
BOTH: From Brillo and stern daffodil

ROSEMARY: And now we'd better change, they'll be arriving
soon
If providence is generous they'll prove a perfect
boon
HERBERT: The dog will be fed
ROSEMARY: And she'll make the bed
HERBERT: Each morning will anticipate a peaceful afternoon
[*Door bell rings.*]

HERBERT: Good God, it's she
ROSEMARY: or he
HERBERT: Or both, you change, I'll stay and see

[ROSEMARY *looks at the pile of newspapers.*]

ROSEMARY: We better tidy up in here
Keep them out until it's clear

> [HERBERT *exits.* ROSEMARY *clears news-
> papers hurriedly and exits with them to kitchen.
> She then hurries off R. For a moment only the
> table occupies the stage. The table chords are
> heard.* HERBERT *looks in and, satisfied that*
> ROSEMARY *has finished, enters with* CHI-

QUITA. *She is a lovely, seductive young thing, the very image of* HERBERT's *fantasy. She carries a small black toolbox which she puts on the sideboard.*]

HERBERT: Here is the dining-room, kitchen over there
CHIQUITA: Excuse me, I didn't mean to stare
[*She has noticed the table.*]
HERBERT: Of course not, there's a good deal to take in
[*He touches her.*]
CHIQUITA [*touches his hand*]:
It's very nice
[*Looks at him.*]
I'm ready to begin.

[*They are suddenly and thoroughly attracted to each other.* HERBERT *looks over his shoulder towards the kitchen from time to time but, all in all, he is quite reckless with* CHIQUITA. *Sultry Latin-American music is heard and they dance together during the following.*]

CHIQUITA: I like it here
The atmosphere is soothing and benign
HERBERT: I'm sure it will be more so with you here
CHIQUITA: It's anodyne

HERBERT: I like your name
Chiquita. Breathing music to the ear
CHIQUITA: Its meant to warm you like an open flame
HERBERT: It does, I fear.
Where did you come from, that makes you so
Like an enchantress?
CHIQUITA: From Mexico
A name of dreams and fire
That makes the passions flow
When melted with desire
They dream of Mexico.

[*They embrace – on the table.*]

HERBERT: I'm glad you've come
Depression flees when you are in the room
CHIQUITA: The tropics always strike depression dumb
HERBERT: And feelings bloom

CHIQUITA: I'm glad to see
You won't be unresponsive to my touch
HERBERT: A similar response takes place in me
CHIQUITA: I thought as much

Things will be better, I'll make them so
Now that I've come here
HERBERT: from Mexico
BOTH: A name of dreams and fire ... [*etc.*]

      [HERBERT *and* CHIQUITA *are now on the table. He is increasingly ardent.*]

HERBERT: How inscrutable the ways of fate
I had despaired of late
Of ever rousing my desire
Or altering its latent state
But now I surge with potent life
You've cut my bonds with love's sweet knife
'Chiquita' sings the lofty choir
      [CHIQUITA *hears a sound.*]
CHIQUITA: Be careful, that may be your wife.

      [*They are instantly on their feet;* HERBERT *puts on his glasses.*]

HERBERT: I'm glad you find it to your taste
The house is quiet, your room well placed
Not too much cooking, we'll be four

      [ROSEMARY *enters, dressed.*]

CHIQUITA: It's a perfect situation – Señor
HERBERT: Well, that is that
      [*To* ROSEMARY]
We've had a chat
ROSEMARY: And how did you get on, you two?

HERBERT: Admirably, I'm sure she'll do

ROSEMARY: Have you seen the house – what is your name?
HERBERT: Chiquita
ROSEMARY: Oh? [*suspiciously.*]
HERBERT: From Mexico
ROSEMARY: How exotic, all the same
    If Herbert is in favour of your staying
    It's settled then ... As I was saying
    Have you seen the house?
CHIQUITA: Except a bit
HERBERT: That is, her bedroom,
CHIQUITA: and the kitchen
ROSEMARY: Then, that's it.
    [ROSEMARY *and* CHIQUITA *– taking her
    toolbox – start off* R.]
    [*Door bell rings.*]
HERBERT: Who's that
ROSEMARY: The gardener, he's coming today
HERBERT: Oh God, of course
    [*As* ROSEMARY *exits with* CHIQUITA]
    I'll be back right away
    [HERBERT *goes to the front door. Once again
    the table is the only person on the stage. Table
    chords.
    After a moment* HERBERT *enters followed by
    * OMAR, *a small swarthy gentleman of some
    mystery and great charm. He carries a suitcase
    and a small black toolbox which he puts on the
    sideboard.*]

HERBERT: Here is the dining-room, kitchen over there
OMAR: Your garden, I noticed, is in dire need of care.

    Things of beauty must be tended
    Or their lustre will be torn
    From them, helpless, undefended
    By the ravages of scorn

[ROSEMARY *enters from the kitchen.*]

ROSEMARY: Chiquita's upstairs. Could you take up her
things?
[OMAR *reacts slightly to 'Chiquita'.*]
Hello, you're the gardener?
[ROSEMARY *is instantly flirtatious.*]

HERBERT: He certainly brings
A clear understanding of gardening skill

OMAR: I may save your garden

ROSEMARY: I'm sure that you will.

HERBERT: We see eye to eye on just what it needs

OMAR: Loam, compost, lime, fertilizer and seeds

HERBERT: Excuse me a moment, you can chat with my wife
[*He exits.*]

ROSEMARY: I would guess that you've led a most interesting
life.

OMAR: Interest abounds if you know how to look.
[HERBERT *enters with* CHIQUITA's *bags and
guitar case.*]

HERBERT: She plays the guitar

ROSEMARY: I hope she can cook
[HERBERT *exits to kitchen.*]
We've hired a new maid, we're so short of time
That we find we need help, the garden's a crime
But now that you're here, by the way what's your
name?

OMAR: Omar, madame,

ROSEMARY: I could tell when you came
That you're not from these parts, you're quite a
new version
Of gardener ... of man

OMAR: Madame, I am Persian
[*Oriental music is heard and, in response to a gest-
ure from* OMAR *the lights dim.*
OMAR *and* ROSEMARY, *like* HERBERT *and*
CHIQUITA *before them, are irresistibly attracted.*

to each other. ROSEMARY'*s behaviour is quite*
abandoned.]

OMAR: I bring a new experience of gardening life
    I come from fabled desert land where centuries of
       strife
    Have cultivated wisdom unlike the pallid bloom
    That flourishes where man believes his castle is a
       room
      [ROSEMARY *takes off her glasses.*]

ROSEMARY: Your fascination glistens in the secrets of your
      eye
    Your darkness may be mystery, but seems to
      vivify
    You see into the soul with your illuminating
      glance
    And understand what others miss, who never
      have the chance

      [*She is on the table, in his arms.*]

OMAR: I open paths through gardens
    Where waste and weeds hold forth
    But fertile temper hardens
    If too long in the North
    You need a touch of passion
    To fructify the soul
    Which doesn't seem the fashion
    As you approach the Pole.

      [*He takes her hand.*]

ROSEMARY: You open paths of joy,
    You open paths of hope,
    For those that grope
    Or fearful stay,
    You make them cope,
    Let instincts play
    And nature's means employ.

OMAR: I open paths through gardens
ROSEMARY: You open paths of joy

OMAR: When fertile tempers harden
      Then *nature's* means employ
      Let's clear the way
      Nor fearful stay
      Let instincts play
ROSEMARY: Oh, fateful day
BOTH: Circumvent the fashion
      With a touch of passion
      Gather rosebuds
      [*They hear a noise.*]
OMAR: Madame, stay
      I think your husband's on the way.

      [*They separate.* ROSEMARY *puts on her glasses.*
      They wait a moment, nothing happens. OMAR,
      shrugging, makes towards ROSEMARY *at the*
      other end of the table. She gives a girlish shriek
      and a chase starts around the table. Chase music.
      OMAR *is a bit half-hearted. Finally he stops,*
      pretending to pant.]

OMAR: It's no use, Madame, let's stop this game
      It's ludicrous.
ROSEMARY: In heaven's name
      What do you mean?
OMAR: You find it tonic
      But for me, this table's marathonic
      I much prefer a normal course
      Your choice is *this*,
       [*indicates table*]
      or my vital force.
OMAR: [*aside*]:
      I hate to resort
      To such a ruse
      But her gay sport
      Is my abuse
      I must drop the seed of doubt
      Assure myself a safe way out
      [*Resumes panting.*]

I'm easily winded, a risk of my profession

ROSEMARY: But Omar, this table's our proudest possession
My husband would never ...

OMAR: It's a simple request
Of course *you* decide.

ROSEMARY: I'll do my best

> [HERBERT *enters. They separate and* OMAR *moves aside.*
> HERBERT *rubs his hands enthusiastically.*]

HERBERT: Well now, she's settled
I think she's a find
Not quickly nettled
Like some of her kind
  She's thoroughly raffiné
  Knows Kirsch from Grand Marnier
  Nutmeg from tarragon
  Clearly a paragon
  Tap-a-tap tim
  Now what about him?

ROSEMARY: From our discussion
He will without doubt
Work like a Prussian
Both inside and out
  We talked of economy
  Covered agronomy
  Touching ecology
  Through agriology
  Tap-a-tap tan
  I'm sure he's our man.

OMAR [*aside*]:
  What bliss she fashions
  Lasciviously
  Her secret passions
  Are focused on me
  She opens her battery
  Rakes me with flattery

Such is my dreary fate
When they hallucinate
Tap-a-tap tat
It's always like that

ROSEMARY: Tap-a-tim
I like him

OMAR: Tap-a-tan
I'm their man

HERBERT: Tap-a-tat
More than that
I've a glorious plan

Paradigm
Tap-a-tim

ROSEMARY: What's your plan
Tap-a-tan

OMAR: And whereat
Tap-a-tat
Tell us all if you can

HERBERT:
Now that we ...

ROSEMARY *and* OMAR:
Let us see,

HERBERT:
Can depend ...

ROSEMARY *and* OMAR:
On a friend?

HERBERT:
On the maid ...

ROSEMARY *and* OMAR:
If she's paid

HERBERT:
Here's the first dividend

ROSEMARY *and* OMAR:
>> For a start ...

HERBERT:
>> She has art ...

ROSEMARY *and* OMAR:
>> She is an ...

HERBERT:
>> Artisan.

ROSEMARY *and* OMAR:
>> You repeat!

HERBERT:
>> So, let's eat

ROSEMARY *and* OMAR:
>> What a staggering plan!

ROSEMARY: Breakfast, what an idea. To think I'd forget.
>> We can have it each morning.

HERBERT: Reading or not

ROSEMARY: Oh, reading! What bliss, no distraction at all

HERBERT: Toast and fried egg will be there when we call
>> Warm and inviting with newspaper waiting
>> [HERBERT *warms up.*]
>> While out in the garden ...

ROSEMARY: the flowers are mating
>> Directed by Omar, who plans their conversion

HERBERT: Omar, you said?

ROSEMARY: Yes, dear, he's Persian
>> [HERBERT *looks at* OMAR *suspiciously.*]

HERBERT: No matter, if Rosemary gives you her blessing
>> No further question enters my mind.
>> [*To* ROSEMARY]
>> If you'll tell Chiquita that hunger is pressing
>> [OMAR *notices* CHIQUITA'*s name again.*]
>> That any delay would be most distressing
>> And that ...

ROSEMARY: don't go on, it's a bit prepossessing
Show him his room.
OMAR: Madame you are kind
HERBERT: What? Oh, yes, quite so
Why don't you come with me
ROSEMARY: *À bientôt*
OMAR: *Madame, je vous en prie.*

[HERBERT *and* OMAR *exit UC.,* ROSEMARY R.

[*Table chords. After a moment* ROSEMARY *re-enters followed by* CHIQUITA *who carries a basket of rolls and a butter dish. She wears a maid's uniform. From the sideboard* ROSEMARY *takes candlesticks etc. and they lay the table ... They do not speak.* ROSEMARY *shows her the silverware in the drawer, napkins, condiments, etc. and indicates that two places are to be laid at either end of the table.* ROSEMARY *then hurries out after* HERBERT *and* OMAR, *leaving* CHIQUITA *on stage. As soon as she is alone,* CHIQUITA *steps into the kitchen and immediately re-enters with her black toolbox.*]

CHIQUITA: Once more alone
Must I search for ever?
Rebuked by fortune, love is still unknown.
She smilingly made me both fair and clever
And endlessly expects me to atone.
She introduces men for me to please
But all, like this one, liabilities.

[*She puts the box on the table.*]

I press my case with all my art
And still no one has touched my heart
Must I play the lonely part
In penance for my beauty?

For paradox I'm well equipped
Abundantly endowed with wit
Ungratefully, I pay for it
Exchanging love for duty.

[*She picks up the toolbox.*]

Once more I need your help, my kit.

> Together we will find the way
> To crush his fancies, bit by bit,
> Enlighten him and save the day ...
> And that will be the end of it.

[She puts her box on the sideboard, starts with astonishment on seeing OMAR's *there, but before she can do anything* ROSEMARY *enters followed by* HERBERT. *He stands at the door admiring* CHIQUITA *who holds* ROSEMARY's *chair for her to sit L. of the table.]*

ROSEMARY: Chiquita, is everything ready?
    Thank you
       [She sits, looks at HERBERT.]
    You're rather unsteady
    Are you well? ...

HERBERT: Just a new situation
    Requiring acclimatization
      *[*CHIQUITA *moves to his chair and holds it back.]*

HERBERT: Oh, thank you Chiquita

CHIQUITA: My pleasure
      [She exits.]

ROSEMARY *[in a loud whisper]*:
    You're right, my dear, she's a treasure

HERBERT: Life has assumed a new hue,
    New interest and zest, thanks to you

ROSEMARY: I tremble with joy I agree
    But the credit is not all to me

HERBERT: A gardener helps, I daresay

ROSEMARY: And a maid, no doubt, lightens the day

[They sit staring at each other, slowly receding into their own thoughts. CHIQUITA *enters with two glasses of fruit juice.* HERBERT *follows her movements avidly. She exits. They sit impassively again.* ROSEMARY *finally fidgets a little and tries to get* HERBERT's *attention.]*

ROSEMARY: Darling, do you think this table's too long?

HERBERT [*Absorbed*]:
    What, my dear, yes, yes, very wrong.
ROSEMARY: That's not what I said
HERBERT: Yes, and quite properly
ROSEMARY: Darling, *please* will you listen to me.
HERBERT: Was there something else you wanted to say?
ROSEMARY: Yes, the table, my dear
HERBERT: Well, have your own way
ROSEMARY: It's too long, I was saying,
HERBERT: The *table* you mean?
ROSEMARY: An exaggeration and *hard* to keep clean
HERBERT: But darling we've eaten for *years* in this way.
ROSEMARY: And I'm *finally* putting my *foot* down, I say
HERBERT: How come it wasn't brought up long ago
           If that's how you felt. It wasn't you know
ROSEMARY: What wasn't brought up?
HERBERT: The table, of course
ROSEMARY: Now darling, there's no need to get cross.

           There were so many things to discuss
           So much on my mind
           Should we travel through Spain
           On the train
           Or the bus
           Should we leave our Dalmatian behind

       [HERBERT *is swept away*.]

HERBERT: Should we spend so much time in the shops
           Should we take *The Times*?
           Should we rent the spare room
           If the boom
           Ever stops?
           Should we substitute lemons for limes?

ROSEMARY: I've never been able
           To bring up the table
           But it's certainly been on my mind

HERBERT: This table's a find
           Like the Cape of Good Horn . . .

ROSEMARY: Hope ...
HERBERT: And your scorn
         Is perverse and unkind.

ROSEMARY: It is so *very* long
         (Could I have the sugar if you please)
         I think it must be wrong
         To eat with such a void between our knees

> [HERBERT *slides the sugar to* ROSEMARY *using a croupier's rake which is slung beneath the table.*]

HERBERT: But, darling, on the whole
         It is handsome, firm and strong
         (Could you pass a roll?)
ROSEMARY: It's too damn long

> [*She slides him a roll with her rake. The discussion becomes very heated.*]

HERBERT: Is this a roll?
ROSEMARY: It looks like one
HERBERT: How very droll
         More like a bun

ROSEMARY: You're just contentious ...
HERBERT: I am sedate
         And conscientious
         In debate!
         I think one must be able,
         In developing a thesis,
         To separately label
         Roll or bun.
         And when we bought the table
         You admired solid pieces ...
ROSEMARY: Let's get a smaller one!
HERBERT: It's not a roll [*looking at it*]
ROSEMARY: It's far too posh [*still referring to the table*]
         It has no soul
HERBERT: It's a species of brioche!
         [ROSEMARY *sighs with irritation.*]

[*They settle in their newspapers while* CHIQUITA
clears the fruit juice. OMAR *enters. He and*
CHIQUITA *see each other and the effect is instan-
taneous. They approach each other, drop to their
knees and, unseen by* ROSEMARY *and* HER-
BERT *crawl under the table to down stage where
they make quiet love.*]

HERBERT: Imagine that, a fellow swam the Channel in
reverse
[*Pause.*]

ROSEMARY: Good God, they've trained a captive dolphin to
converse
[*Pause.*]

HERBERT: Just think, a constantly creating universe
[*Pause.*]

ROSEMARY: Ha! a doctor caught procuring for his nurse
[*Pause.*]

ROSEMARY: Well dear, have we agreed?

HERBERT: Agreed? Of course my love, indeed.

ROSEMARY: We can advertise for buyers next weekend
Unless you'd rather give it to a friend

HERBERT: I'm afraid I've lost the thread . . .

ROSEMARY: Well *con*centrate!
[*Tempers are high.*]
We've both agreed to *sell* at any rate

HERBERT: If you're talking of the table I don't agree at all
Whatever could replace it is ridiculously small
This is a thing of beauty – *in corpore sano*!

[*Pause.*]

ROSEMARY: How about a piano?
[HERBERT *hesitates.*]

HERBERT: Well, I'm very fond of music – but I like the
table more
You were thoroughly delighted when we saw it
in the store.

ROSEMARY: That was years ago, but now . . . We never meet

We sit across the Persian Gulf, every time we eat.

HERBERT: The Persian Gulf, oh dear, you're wrong
The Gulf of Mexico.

ROSEMARY: The Persian Gulf my dear is long ...
Full of tankers don't you know
As for the Gulf of Mexico, it's round

HERBERT: That may be true
Still it's dotted with islands, like salt and pepper,
Sugar and candlesticks too!

ROSEMARY: Candlesticks? Darling, I'm sure that's not so
Not in the Gulf of Mexico.

HERBERT: It's dotted with candlesticks, look at a map

ROSEMARY: Oh, no you don't. You're laying a trap
[*She rings a bell on the table.*]
But there is someone here who will certainly
know.
[CHIQUITA *rises, downstage of table.*]
Chiquita are there candlesticks in the Gulf of
Mexico?

HERBERT: Chiquita I forbid you to reply to this tirade
So this is why you had to have a Mexican maid
Sometimes you go too far
[*He calls.*]
Omar,
[OMAR *rises.*]

OMAR: Sir,

HERBERT: Oh, there you are
Now reason will prevail, Omar we want to know
Would you rather eat on the Persian Gulf or the
Gulf of Mexico?

ROSEMARY: Herbert, I object, you can't use our Persian
gardener this way

HERBERT: Why not?

OMAR: Why not, indeed, I've a great deal to say
Let me tell you a fable learned in my childhood

CHIQUITA: How delightful, a story

OMAR: Shall I tell it?

HERBERT, ROSEMARY *and* CHIQUITA: Yes

OMAR: Good.
[*They listen attentively.*]

OMAR [*sitting on the table; music is heard*]:
> Once there was a king
> Who had three chests
> One gold, one silver, one bronze.
>
> One day a suitor arrived to ask
> For the hand of the Princess.
> [CHIQUITA *joins him on the table.*]
> A handsome and capable young man he was
> And the king granted his request
> So the happy couple rode off together
> [*He takes* CHIQUITA's *hand.*]
> Several years later
> The king died
> Without ever learning what was in the three
> chests.
> [OMAR *and* CHIQUITA *kiss.*]

CHIQUITA: Ah, we have a story . . . much like that too
It makes the same point

OMAR: Will you tell it

ROSEMARY *and* HERBERT: Yes, d

CHIQUITA [*Music*]:
> Once a soldier returned from the wars
> And met a fair young girl
> And immediately he fell in love.
>
> He asked her to marry him
> She refused and said
> That she had waited seven long years
> For her true love to return from the wars
> And she will wait forever if need be
>
> The soldier rode off
> And the girl lived and died
> Unmarried.
> [*They kiss again.*]

CHIQUITA: So tell me, my fox
       [she points to the sideboard]
       Is that your box?

OMAR: It's mine, I must admit
       [He looks at sideboard and sees CHIQUITA'S *box.]*
       Good God, a duplicate
       Yours, my Persian cat?

CHIQUITA: Yes, my desert rat.
       [Kiss.]

HERBERT *[to* ROSEMARY*]*:
       Can you make any sense of *that* remark?

ROSEMARY: I'm completely in the dark.

HERBERT: Well, I hardly think the subject can be closed

ROSEMARY: Nothing's settled . . .

OMAR *[standing on the table]*: Wrong, I am exposed
              I'm not your Persian gardener,
                never could be.

HERBERT: Why didn't you tell us that before?

ROSEMARY: Why should he?

OMAR: You never asked the question

HERBERT: I do now, by God
       [He mounts the table, faces OMAR.*]*

ROSEMARY: Herbert, calm, now Omar, do you think this
       table odd?

OMAR: Shall I make a suggestion?

HERBERT: Yes, tell us who you are

OMAR: That was not her question

HERBERT: It's the best we have so far

OMAR *[tearing up newspapers]*:
       You have to know everything, don't you?
       You'll be furious otherwise, won't you?
       Why ball bearings are round
       Why the interest's compound
       On the money the savings bank loan'd you

CHIQUITA *[tearing up newspapers]*:
       Why Socrates went without sandals
       Why catfish have whiskery handles

Why does tin oxydize
Can machines synthezise
Were the Goths any kin to the Vandals?

OMAR: Do I have the floor?

CHIQUITA: Yes, dear, you do.

OMAR [*to* HERBERT]:
Well then, I'm no more
A gardener than you.

HERBERT: You're what?

ROSEMARY: You're not?

HERBERT: You're what?

ROSEMARY: You're not?

OMAR: No more a gardener than you.

ROSEMARY: And are you a deception too,
A spurious maid, Chiquita?

CHIQUITA: Exactly so,
I wouldn't know
An egg cup from an egg beater!

HERBERT: We've been used!

ROSEMARY: Impertinent ingratitude!

HERBERT: Confidence abused!

ROSEMARY: Diabolic latitude!
Pretending that I mattered all the while
And furtively you sought Chiquita's smile

HERBERT [*to* CHIQUITA]:
And now you think this jelly-fish worth landing
Overtures to me notwithstanding

CHIQUITA: They were empty, worthless declarations
As feckless as the passions of crustaceans

OMAR [*to* ROSEMARY]:
While you, your pallid soul and flaccid taste
Addressed to *me* were utterly misplaced.

HERBERT [*to* ROSEMARY]:
Outrageous deceit!
This girl masqueraded for me
As the image of my fantasy
A shimmering will-o'-the-wisp

Serving ardour with love's languid lisp

ROSEMARY [*to* HERBERT]:
Imposture complete!
This man masqueraded for me
As the secret of love's sorcery
Fulfilment of tremulous hope
With whom I could gladly elope.

HERBERT: She was the Pygmalion of my atelier of dreams
ROSEMARY: He, the moonlit vision at the garden's furthest
reach
HERBERT: And now she's real, it seems
ROSEMARY: While he, this *girl* esteems,
HERBERT: Excluding me,
ROSEMARY: Excluding me,
BOTH: A bitter, painful breach;

HERBERT: My disappointment burns me.
ROSEMARY: My perfect lover spurns me.

ROSEMARY: This mockery shocks
HERBERT: Even more than it mocks
We've been taken in I'm afraid
ROSEMARY: A gardener indeed
He's a fraudulent breed
HERBERT: And she, we can see, is no maid.

HERBERT: What are you?
ROSEMARY: WHAT ARE YOU?
BOTH: WHAT ARE YOU?

OMAR: Illusion smashers
CHIQUITA: Table crashers
OMAR: Exterminators
CHIQUITA: Fumigators
OMAR: Stern reprovers
CHIQUITA [*indicates table*]:
Bulk removers
OMAR: Settlers of indigestion
HERBERT: At last, they've answered my question!

OMAR: And for the first time I've met a fellow spirit.
                [CHIQUITA *and* OMAR *embrace.*]
HERBERT [*drily*]:
                As you see, I'm delighted to hear it.
OMAR: After years of working alone
                I've met another rebellious vision
                I would claim her for my own
                I wait, impatient for her decision
CHIQUITA [*to* OMAR]:
                Before I consider the course you demand
                I think we should finish the business on hand
OMAR: Right, to work – my kit if you please
                [CHIQUITA *gets his box.*]
                I'll set it up if you'll remove these
                [*He indicates things to be cleared off the table.*
                CHIQUITA *does so and gets her box.*

                HERBERT *crosses under table to* ROSEMARY
                while CHIQUITA *and* OMAR *are unlocking their*
                boxes.]

HERBERT: Rosemary, this is completely out of hand
                We must know at once where we stand.
ROSEMARY: I'm baffled, this never happened before
                We'll just have to wait and see what's in store

                [*They sit at either end of the table. During this*
                OMAR *and* CHIQUITA *have opened their boxes.*
                OMAR *has removed a portable electric circular*
                saw and with CHIQUITA'S *help he saws the*
                table in half. Sawdust fills the air. ROSEMARY
                and HERBERT *cover their ears while the saw*
                rips through the table and then burst into tears
                when the table crashes to the ground. CHIQUITA
                produces handkerchiefs from her box which she
                hands them to dry their eyes.]

HERBERT [*rising*]:
                Now that he's done this

[*to* ROSEMARY]
Would you share his pillow?

ROSEMARY [*rising*]:
I renounce that bliss,
And shrink from peccadillo!
But, now that she's exposed,
Is she still your Dido?

HERBERT: That affair is closed
I've muzzled my libido

CHIQUITA [*to* HERBERT]:
And I would suggest that you pardon her
It was only a harmless effusion
He's irresistible this Persian gardener
Planter of doubt and confusion

ROSEMARY [*timidly*]:
I pardon you.

HERBERT [*nobly*]:
I pardon you!

[*They embrace.*]

HERBERT: Meanwhile we have things to do
ROSEMARY: Things that need attending to
HERBERT: Heaven knows when we'll be through
ROSEMARY: That's how it seems to me

OMAR: We can leave you on your own
Confronted by the great unknown

CHIQUITA: From little seeds are tables grown
Which once had been a tree!

[OMAR *and* CHIQUITA *slip away.* ROSE-
MARY *and* HERBERT *have taken pencils and
paper during the above and have been writing.
They read what they have written.*]

ROSEMARY: Wanted, young, attractive maid ...
HERBERT: Wanted, handy, willing gardener ...
ROSEMARY: For small house ...

HERBERT: For small garden ...
ROSEMARY: Live in, no children.
HERBERT: Some knowledge of carpentry ... desirable.

CURTAIN

HEATHCOTE WILLIAMS

The Local Stigmatic

The Local Stigmatic was first presented with *The Dwarfs*, by Harold Pinter, at the Traverse Theatre, on 1 March 1966, with the following cast:

GRAHAM, *a man in his mid-twenties*   Oliver Cotton
RAY, *a man in his mid-twenties*   William Hoyland
MAN IN THE STREET   Toby Salaman
DAVID, *a man in his middle thirties*   Peter Hill

Directed by PETER GILL

The Local Stigmatic was subsequently presented at the Royal Court Theatre, on 27 March 1966, with the same cast.

A room. Late afternoon. Winter. GRAHAM *is standing.* RAY *is
sitting.*

GRAHAM: ... I'm in with Hancox the trainers, Ray, that's
what he SAID. Look, Ray, he got me by the elbow. Messing
about. Moving the flesh about on it, SEE Ray. I was just
going in, I had my three and six ready. Come over here, he
said to me, I'm in with Hancox the trainers, and I'll give
you two, Ray, two for the third race. You'll just make it.
So, Ray, I pulled out an inordinately large sum of money
which he immediately grabbed, you see, and he gave me
Hermosa of Selsdon as number one, and Polish Otto.
Hermosa of Selsdon, Ray. Do it on the forecast, do it on
the tote, he said. So I went in and shelled out ten shillings
on Hermosa of Selsdon and the other dog, and then I came
out front and watched how the betting was going. Hermosa
of Selsdon was ten to one, you see Ray. Well, I didn't know
what the dividend might be, Ray, so I shelled out a couple
of sheets on it there with some egg ... AND ALL THIS
TIME, Ray, all this time there was this faithless mob shelling
out on a dog called Mystic Nora ... but I don't know why,
Ray, I don't know why, this fellow had instilled faith into
me, I don't know why ...

RAY: Go on.

GRAHAM: I trusted him, Ray, just because he'd ... come up.
Well, the fanfares blew and they brought them out and
this fellow I was with said: There's yours. There's your dog,
Hermosa of Selsdon. So I looked at it, and I swear, Ray,
when I looked back again they'd lengthened to fourteens.
I thought everyone's gone MAD, Ray, everyone's gone
MAD ... and then you won't believe this Ray, I was
watching this dog, you see, and they walked it round and
back again, and just as they were putting this dog into the
trap, it stopped dead in its tracks, shivered, then it tightened

171

up, then it lowered its little arse, then it had the mother an‹
father of all dumps. It was standing at only fifty-two pound
as it was, but after that lot had shot through its glory hole
it was nearer forty ...

RAY: Won't make much difference.

GRAHAM: Of course it does, Ray. That's how to catch ou‹
those eggs in the ring. They've got their backs to the dog
and the dog's psychology. Anyhow, Ray, they get them i›
and the bell goes and the hare comes shooting round, set
off the traps, and some bloody egg behind me shouts
They're off.

RAY: I KNOW.

GRAHAM: Well, to cut it short for you, Ray, it was this do‹
Mystic Nora all the way. Hermosa of Selsdon wasn't in i‹
Nowhere. Dead out, Ray. I just STARED, you know, jus
STARED. And when they came onto the track to take ›
off, Ray, then it didn't want to GO. That's what really g‹
me, Ray, IT DIDN'T WANT TO GO ... IT DIDN'›
WANT TO GO ... I tell you, Ray, I wanted to get dow›
there and kick it to death. I ... I ... I saw that dog fo‹
what it really was ... just a ... just a dirty little whippet ..
just a bowlegged dachshund on stilts ... filthy little fa‹
with a horse-hair shirt ... stop it from gassing everyone ..

RAY: Yes. I don't usually bother with the forecast actually
Usually double up on the favourites. Very fair last Thurs
day as a matter of fact, Graham. I used to do the Duell
pools sometimes on the off chance, but they closed it dow›
for forecast betting ...

GRAHAM: Yes ... yes, well anyway I'm talking about las
Saturday at Wandsworth, Ray. So, we were just going yo‹
see, when this fellow I went with turned to me and said
What are you going to do? About that fellow at the gate
I'd completely forgotten about him Ray. So, we walke‹
back up the stands, and he's in the bar with his back to us
This fellow I was with is a bloody egg in fact: do you kno›
what he did, Ray? He just burnt a cigarette hole in the bac‹
of his coat. Just like that. Then he taps him on the shoulde‹
and says: Hello. So the fellow turns round then, Ray, an‹

he doesn't recognize us at first, and then he does: Oh yes, he says, hello boys, have a drink, have a drink. So this fellow I'm with, Ray, Jimmy ... he ... Jimmy says: Two double scotches. He gets them. He gets them, and then this fellow I was with grabs him and he says: Ay wonder if you could help me. Ay'm eager to recoup certain losses made recently in an ill-advaysed venture, and Ay have here this tin of Elastoplast which Ay'm interested in selling. In fact, I sell it so cheap, that ... it ... would ... be a pleasure to cut yourself ...

RAY: Heard that before. Huh.

GRAHAM: SO, Ray, so this half-hard idiot who gave us the dogs gradually catches on that he's being threatened, and he shoots his mouth off, you see, and we get thrown out. They wouldn't let us back in. You know, I know one of the fellows there: works as a hatch clerk. Always has half a dollar on trap six whether there's a dog in it or not. HE wouldn't let us back in.

RAY: Oh well. You had a good day. Shouldn't let it worry you. [*Gets up and goes to the window. Opens it. Pause.*] Graham. Do you remember the time I was barred from that queer pub in Earls Court for adjusting the vertical hold on the television set?

GRAHAM: Yes, Ray.

RAY: That was ironical, wasn't it; barred from a queer pub for adjusting the vertical hold ...

GRAHAM: Yes. Oh go and unravel in the bath. You're getting like Aunty Daisy, you are, pushing out the dirt ... THAT BLOODY DOG ... THAT BLOODY LITTLE ANIMAL ...

RAY: Oh forget it.

GRAHAM: I have forgotten it.

RAY: You've forgotten about forgetting it as well.

GRAHAM: OH YES. YES.

[*Pause.*]

Listen, it's under two years old; it was whelped by Thermic Rays from Keneally Friend. July thirty-first, five hundred yards, trap four, normal running: fast away, ran wide, every chance, finished second. Beaten by Tarry No Dividend. August the fifth, five hundred yards, normal running, trap six, ran and finished well, Ray; first. August the twelfth, five hundred yards, normal running, trap two, badly baulked, finished well, second, beaten by Breeks Rambler, Ray, Breeks Rambler ...

[RAY *sits down.*]

RAY: I don't know.

GRAHAM: What? Don't know what?

RAY: Got out of bed the wrong side.

GRAHAM: It must have done.

RAY: I did.

GRAHAM: Oh did you, RIGHT, then ... RIGHT. RIGHT. [*Pause.*] Sharon ... she coming round ... bringing any food?

RAY: I didn't ask her to. I didn't give her any money.

GRAHAM: I never pay for sex Ray, because Jesus Christ paid for our sins.

RAY: That's got nothing to do with it.

GRAHAM: I like her Ray. I like her very much.

RAY: Let's give her a miss. Let's go up the West End.

[GRAHAM *stands up.*]

GRAHAM: Right then ... What's the name of that place you got thrown out of. Let's go there.

RAY: Earl of Strathmore ... Strathcona ... that's in Earls Court.

GRAHAM: Oh. Close that bloody window. [*Walks across the room. Picks up a paper.*]

[RAY *stays at the window.*]

GRAHAM [*reading*]: 'With railers drawn on the outside and wide runners on the inside, tonight's heats of the Ben Truman stakes at New Cross present a really difficult assignment for punters and I would not be at all surprised to see more than a couple of shocks before the six for Saturday's finals are known ...' What do they want to do that for? Balingaddy runs WIDE. They should shove it on the outside. She's a very pacy little hound. Clocked 28.06 solo last Monday. Remember? They've written it up:

'She is also no stranger to New Cross having won over the course and distance, and connexions were wise to renew her associations with the circuit by giving her a five hundred yards spin on Monday ...' She'll be on big offer.

AY: She won't be on big offer at all. What you say that for?

RAHAM: She's got Miss Vanilla and Spring Guest against her.

AY: Huh. Half an hour's boredom and agony for a few seconds' pleasure.

RAHAM: If Sharon was here she'd say: that's like a lot of things Ray, and leer at you. I've spared you that.

AY: How bothered was I about being spared it.

RAHAM: It's all on the cards.

AY: I don't see it.

RAHAM: Oh well it doesn't matter. I'm not going that far with you.

he same day. Evening. VOICE OFF [*Commissionaire*]: '*Seven and x, standing room only. Seven and six standing. You'll have to wait, rry, you have to wait. Standing room only.*' VOICE *recedes. Traffic ises recede.* RAY *and* GRAHAM *walking. Fade up.*

RAHAM [*putting on his coat*]: I remember coming out of the pictures with one fellow and we walked the whole way to Holborn Viaduct, and he didn't say a word, and then he turned to me and he said: Well, those Italians really know what life is about. I could have kicked him in the crutch.

AY: The last time I went to the pictures with you, you said you went with some American and after you came out he said: Some very poignant songs have come from the mines.

RAHAM: I could have cut his balls off too.

AY: I remembered your saying that. Came from Pittsburgh. Huh. I remembered that. There aren't any bloody mines in Pittsburgh.

RAHAM: Not IN Pittsburgh, Ray, no. But as far as I remember, Ray, Pittsburgh's the centre of the mining district in Pennsylvania. I forced that out of him. Let's go

and have a drink Ray. [*Pause.*] My nerves are bloody woun
up.

RAY: I could drink you under the table.

GRAHAM: Have to be a small table.

RAY: Huh. You're getting very kittenish.

GRAHAM: Ha. Let's go and have a drink Ray. [*Pause.*] What'
the nearest pub you were thrown out of.

RAY: We've passed it.

GRAHAM: Which one was that.

RAY: Strathmore Arms. The barman came over to me an
said: You'll have to go. I'm sorry you'll have to go.

GRAHAM: Why.

RAY: You're always reading. You bore the customers.

GRAHAM: You're always reading. You bore the customers.

RAY: Huh.

GRAHAM: Let's go there.

[*Third set of footsteps approaches. Undisciplined.* MAN *walk
across between* RAY *and* GRAHAM.]

GRAHAM: Hello there. How's it going then?

MAN [*turning slowly*]: ... hello.

[MAN *leaves. Footsteps recede.*]

RAY: Who was that. Are you playing your game.

GRAHAM [*looking down the street*]: That turned him over. Le
him cook on the other side.

RAY: He didn't look that sort to me. For a start he was cut t
pieces and reeling around the street. You could have pisse
in his face and watched it evaporate.

GRAHAM: Right. You don't believe me Ray. Turn round
we'll catch him up.

[GRAHAM *runs back.* RAY *walks back.*]

GRAHAM: Hello then.

MAN [*reappearing*]: YOU'RE NOT JOSEPH AT ALL ..

GRAHAM [*to* RAY]: There you go. [*To* MAN] I've seen you a
Catford Dog Track, haven't I.

MAN: You're NOT JOSEPH AT ALL ... GET OUT
OF MY FUCKING WAY ... I never go to the Grey
hound ... Racing Association ... I have ... OTHE

things to do. Come here, come here ... you ... you ...
know what Winston Churchill said about dogs. I'll tell you
that. You read that before you ... you go on to me
ABOUT THAT ...

[GRAHAM *reaches out at him*.]

Don't you touch me. I have EVERY RIGHT to walk
up and down here without you fucking West End drug
addicts coming up to me. [*Goes over to* RAY.] You know what
Winston Churchill said about dogs. He said they were
ANIMATED ROULETTE. He had ALL THE
WIT IN THE WORLD ... That'll keep you thinking
for a bit. [*Turning to face* GRAHAM.] What you come up to
me for? Why don't you ... why don't you just walk about
the streets with RAYS COMING OUT OF YOUR
EYES, and RAYS coming out of the tips of your fingers
... that's what you're at, and LEAVE ME ALONE ...
you DAMN WELL GO AWAY ... DAMN WELL
GO AWAY ...

GRAHAM [*crouching*]: What a naughty little man, Ray, he's
trying to break the rules ... You might have been a man
who gave me a tip last week. I might have wanted to thank
you for it, or kick you to death. Hermosa of Selsdon at
twenty to one?

RAY: What are you talking about Graham.

GRAHAM: Hermosa of Selsdon at twenty to one?

MAN: Well I want no thanks from you, and when I want to
thank you for something, I shan't ... He had ALL THE
WIT IN THE WORLD ... DAMN WELL GO
AWAY ... bloody split-arse ruining the bloody streets ...
get out ...

GRAHAM: Hermosa of Selsdon at twenty to one?

MAN: Get out.

GRAHAM: Get out.

[MAN *slouches off*.]

ooooooooeeeeeee! OOOOOOOEEEEEEEE! Hermosa
of Selsdon ... at twenty to one? ... HERMOSA OF
SELSDON ... AT TWENTY TO ONE? ...
OOOOOO ... EEEEEEE! HERM ... O ... SA

... OF ... SELS ... DON ... AT ... TWEN ... TY
... TO ... WER ... ERN ... HERMO ... SA ... OF
SELS ... DON ... AT ... TWEN ... TY ... TC
... WER ... ERN ...

[*Pause.*]

RAY: If you say: You see what I mean, I think I'll go quietly
mad.

GRAHAM: Look, the next time, you BLOODY GC
ALONG WITH ME.

RAY: That dog didn't win.

GRAHAM: Oh God, Ray, I give up. YOU BLOODY GC
ALONG WITH ME. BLOODY GO ALONG
WITH ME RAY.

[*Pause.*]

RAY: He was shaking all over.

GRAHAM: It's all very well your saying you'll go quietl
mad, if I say: You see what I mean ...

RAY: Poor old bastard. For all you know his wife might jus
have died, or he might have been laid off or something ..

GRAHAM: Oh for crying out loud Ray. Laid off ...

[*Pause.*]

GRAHAM [*quietly*]: You see what I mean. I'll fucking well sa
it now.

RAY: What? Let's go in here.

A bar.

RAY: A scotch, and a glass of tonic with a slice of lemo
Thanks. [*Brings the drinks to the table.*]

GRAHAM: How much thought did you give it.

RAY: What.

GRAHAM: Hermosa of Selsdon.

RAY: Oh. I didn't pay much attention to it. I had Fairlan
Mandy and Matson Wonder. Fairlands Mandy can catc
pigeons.

GRAHAM: That wasn't very adventurous of you.

RAY: One of the selections said Hermosa of Selsdon would be a back marker most of the way.

GRAHAM: That's a bloody lie.

RAY: It was in Thursday's *Greyhound Express*.

GRAHAM: Here you are then, I've got the bloody cutting. You find it then. GO ON YOU BLOODY WELL FIND IT.

[*Pause.*]

RAY: What's that.

GRAHAM: *Weekend.* Huh.

RAY [*reading*]: 'How would you spend your last hour? *Weekend* asked sixteen famous people what they would do – given the choice – as the seconds ticked away: Sixty Minutes to Live ...' What would you do?

GRAHAM: I'D READ THE BLOODY THING. IF I SAID I WAS GOING TO READ THE BLOODY THING I'D READ THE BLOODY THING.

RAY: 'One hour to live. Sixty minutes left on earth to wind up the account. Many men have faced up to it. Some bravely. Some with a whimper. It is about the most profound subject a human being can think about. But it is only when people start talking about those vital sixty minutes that the infinite variety of views emerges. Would you pray? Would you cry? Would you leave with a smile? You, alone, know ...'

GRAHAM: What do they say then.

RAY: I think it's interesting. 'During those last few minutes TV personality Katie Boyle would be ...'

GRAHAM: Oh BELT UP ... I don't want to hear it ... I don't ...

RAY: '... she'd be tearing up old love letters and destroying other correspondences. She said "I've always saved all my letters – they're tied in neat bundles ..."'

GRAHAM: I said shut up didn't I.

RAY: I think it's interesting. [*Leans across and stares at* GRAHAM.] Don't you Graham. '... in neat bundles with blue satin ribbons – and I shouldn't like to leave anything behind that might hurt anybody.' But the bonfire of beribboned letters would have to wait until Katie Boyle had made arrangements to have her two miniature Pekes: Mi-Tzi and Tai-Tai taken off ... taken care of ...'

GRAHAM: Oh GOD, Ray.

RAY: I think it's interesting. 'The future prospects of personal pets would be the first concern of writer Beverly Nichols. "I would ask Gaskin, my man servant, to take care of my three cats: Anthony Trollope and Five ..."'—that's only two, Graham, that's only two cats.

GRAHAM: That's the price you have to pay isn't it. It's THREE, you silly cunt: Anthony, Trollope and Five .. Three.

RAY: 'I would then give Gaskin the time off, and I would play some records: Rachmaninov's 18th variation on a theme by ...' You've read it then.

GRAHAM: Yes.

RAY: Well, what you on about, why can't I read it.

GRAHAM: I'm not stopping you. YOU GO AHEAD AND BLOODY READ IT THEN.

RAY: All right, I will.

GRAHAM: I couldn't give a bugger what you do.
    [*Pause.*]

RAY: As a matter of fact there are a lot of people you follow in here: Anna Massey, Jimmy Hill, the Duke of Bedford, Shirley Ann Field ... 'What would be the last fling of socialite Mrs Bunty Kinsman? A parachute jump over the Sussex Downs to buy two gorgeous dresses from Balenciaga.' I'm just picking on the funny ones, Graham. For a laugh.

GRAHAM: Yes.

RAY: Didn't you say you met her.

GRAHAM: No ... no ... I don't know, Jesus Christ.
    [*Pause.*]

RAY: Oh, it's got beer all over it. You don't want it do you Graham? Might as well leave it here.

GRAHAM: Let's go, Ray, let's go down the road.

RAY [*leaning forward, coldly*]: I didn't read you out the best one

Graham. Barbara Cartland, the famous novelist, she said, when her last hour came, she'd stay busy spending the rest of her time labelling little mementos 'To Emily', 'To Aggie', 'To Tommy', 'To Richard', and all her dearest friends, and this would avoid her executors having to do it, and stop the wrong things going to the wrong people ... I shouldn't have thought it would matter much. I should have thought she could mix up all her friends and all of her things together and nobody'd know the difference ...

GRAHAM: LOOK YOU CAN GO BACK TO THAT OLD COW OF YOURS IF YOU LIKE. You don't have to come out with me, you know ... and what with her minge and your socks you'll HAVE to open the fucking window. Just bloody go along with me, that's all. Bloody go along with me. You can go off home if you like and if she's not there, you can go and have a row with yourself in the toilet, go and unravel in the bath. I don't care. I tell you I don't ... I tell you ... I tell you ...

RAY: No, I just thought. I mean, I like going out with you, Graham.

GRAHAM: Yes.

RAY: You ... you ... It's all right with you, Graham.

GRAHAM: Yes it is, oh yes, Ray. Yes, you're quite right Ray. Oh yes.

[*Pause.*]

GRAHAM: Listen to this prick [*reading*]: 'Hermosa of Selsdon has more than an average turn of early foot, and from a favourable draw may well reach the first bend in front, should sweep away into the lead and career away for what could well be the most decisive winning margin of the evening. Great Gusto as his name implies is a stout finisher and if he can avoid trouble should outstay all but the selection: Hermosa of Selsdon ...' How they have the NERVE to bring that dog up again ... we've SEEN that bloody hound ... SEEN that bloody hound ... 'favoured by having trap three vacant'. It wouldn't make any difference if they were all vacant ... we've *seen* that bastard dog.

RAY: Isn't that him? That one.

GRAHAM: Who. Wouldn't make any difference if they were all bloody vacant. Who, who. What's the time.

RAY [*pointing*]: One of those people you follow. There. No, *there*. You see, there. THERE. There he is. There, there he goes, see him. There he goes. Quick. Just behind the . . . THERE HE IS . . .

GRAHAM: Yes. Yes. No, it's not the one you're . . . Ray. It's another . . . one. I know who you mean. I know who he is. Yes.

    [*Slight pause.*]

RAY: Well, let's go and chat him up.

GRAHAM: Yes, Ray. Whatever for, Ray.

RAY: Well, then the next time you see him you can say to yourself, well . . . you know, that you and me chatted him up, Graham, and how it went or something. I don't know. I don't know why you follow those people.

GRAHAM: They follow me. Going along with me, are you?

RAY: Yes, well yes. Yes, Graham.

GRAHAM: You're being a bit kittenish.

RAY: Graham.

    [RAY *and* GRAHAM *leave.*]

Another table in the bar. DAVID *is sitting down with a Campari.* GRAHAM *and* RAY *take up positions by the table. Pause.*

GRAHAM: Excuse me, I'd just like to say I admired the way you extricated yourself from that dirty little bitch on the train to Santa Fé.

DAVID [*looking up*]: Oh . . . oh, you . . . OH yes . . . you . . . saw that, did you. Yes, yes.

GRAHAM: Yes, my friend and I happened to spot you in the corner and we thought you wouldn't mind if we came over and let you know that we were on your side.

DAVID: Oh, well, huh . . . yes, well, thank you . . . they're . . . they're releasing it again as a matter of fact. I was very pleased about that. I mean you're probably . . .

GRAHAM: Oh no, David, we'll be there. We'll be there.

DAVID: Yes. I thought that was fairly well buried that ... nice you should ...

GRAHAM: Oh no, we're great admirers of yours. Do you know, David, do you know where we first saw you. You had a part you wouldn't spit on now in *Oklahoma* at Hastings. Five years ago. There's not many people come up to you David, and say that.

DAVID: No ... no ... huh ... funny ... remember that ... very well. Local paper said it was a once-in-a-lifetime-clinch-with-gaiety ... huh.

GRAHAM: That's a giggle, isn't it, Ray. Can we get you a drink? You couldn't have carried on there, singing she was the fisherman's daughter and her place was covered in crabs. Not your style, David.

RAY: Drink?

DAVID: Oh ... well, Campari.

GRAHAM: I'll get it. Don't want to rush you off your feet Ray. Campari ... that's port and lemon in disguise. You're sewn up, aren't you? [*Leaving.*] Campari, scotch and a glass of tonic with a slice of lemon. You know the old joke, don't you David.

[GRAHAM *leaves.* RAY *sits down in the chair next to* DAVID. *Stares at him.*]

GRAHAM [*coming back*]: She's been taken up hasn't she, that dirty bitch in the train to Santa Fé.

DAVID: Oh ... yes ... she's been ... thank you ... she's been taken up in a big way ... Oh, yes ...

GRAHAM [*sitting down*]: Tell me David, this recent one you've been working on ... what's the director like to work with?

DAVID: Oh, you've been reading about that one, have you? Very difficult going to begin with, but I found that the only way to avoid a direct clash ... personalities ... was to ... well ... *almost exactly* the opposite to what he wanted. Not *quite* the exact opposite you see ... do you see what I mean, but *almost* the exact opposite. And then you see, he *knew* that you weren't kowtowing to him like everyone else, and at the same time you weren't sort of ... playing the game of doing the exact opposite in order to show that you were *obviously*, as it were, standing up to him ... you see ... very ...

GRAHAM: Brilliant, David, absolutely BRILLIANT. Ray.

RAY: Yes, Graham, very, very clever.
[*Pause.*]

GRAHAM: Funny, Ray and I were talking about that film just before ... and he bet you lived it up there, David.

DAVID: Yes, well ... no ... it's not what you'd ... you'd imagine ... at all really.

GRAHAM: Oh NO, we've got no ILLUSIONS about it. No illusions at all. I can imagine just what it's like, you know. They don't keep you at arm's length. It's all written up. I saw you rehearsing the other day in Hammersmith, some hall there. I was passing by, I know a fellow who works there.

DAVID: Really? Jesus, that'd be the new ...

GRAHAM: Oh yes, David, we often pass that place on the way to the dogs. Do you ever go to the dogs at all?

DAVID: No ... I don't, I'm afraid ... Never have the time ... I ... I ... I'd lose ... suppose ... How do they work it exactly? Have a hare, mechanical hare ... someone said about the greyhound racing? Some remark. I was reading it the other day. Animated roulette. Winston Churchill ... animated roulette. Huh. No I don't follow it really.

RAY: Graham follows it.

DAVID: Yes. [*Pause.*] Be with you in a minute ... just going downstairs to shake the icicles off. Huh. [*Goes through to the stairs leading to the toilet.*]

RAY: He's gone downstairs, Graham. See a man about a dog. Huh.
[*Silence.*]

GRAHAM: Are you going along with me ... you going to hedge your bet.
[*Silence.*]

RAY: No, Graham, no. It's what you say. Just what you say. The old black magic.
[*Silence.*
DAVID *comes back.*]

RAY [*standing up, to* GRAHAM]: Who's the third man who walks
   beside you?

DAVID: Hello. Huh.

GRAHAM: Knock them back, don't you David. I bet your
   liver goes on living long after you're dead; you'll have to
   employ someone like us to come over and beat it to death.
   [*Standing up.*] What about coming down the road with us;
   place we know.

DAVID: No. Really I've ... I've got to get back. I really must
   get back ... very, very tired ...

GRAHAM: We'll walk along with you.

Traffic sounds. An alley. Traffic sounds fade out. Fade up.

GRAHAM: You haven't let us introduce ourselves: my name's
   Graham, David. This is my very good friend, Ray Summers
   ... Do you mind being recognized by strangers?

DAVID: Oh ... it's just part of ... depends who they are ...
   they usually get my name wrong, and then they get embarrassed and walk off ... doesn't take much out of you.

GRAHAM: I expect a lot of them ask you for your autograph
   and say it's for their small son, or their nephew, someone
   you've never heard of to cover up.

DAVID: Yes, yes ... funny you should say that, I was ...

GRAHAM: Can I have your autograph. It's for Ray.
   [DAVID *takes the book.*]

RAY: You've got one of those pens that writes underwater.

DAVID: Oh ... huh ... I never knew they ... useful for
   playing the ... the Duke of ... Duke of ... Clarence ... huh.

GRAHAM: They wouldn't let you. He was Jewish. There were
   fifty thousand Sephardic Jews in England in ten sixty six.
   They all got to the top and then nobody knew who they
   were. There were twenty thousand Negroes in England in
   the eighteen hundreds and nobody knows where they are
   either. Ray's Jewish. He had to have it cut off, and I bloody
   wore it off.
   [DAVID *laughs.*]

GRAHAM: Stop laughing. You sound like a clam going mad

DAVID: Oh, huh ... yes ... Well, I must ...

GRAHAM: We turn down here.

DAVID: Well, perhaps I'll run across you again ...

GRAHAM: Run across us again. You'll have to run very ver
fast, David. Very very fast. Don't you live in Knightsbridg
now, David. I saw your house in Chiswick was up for sa
... in the property column.

DAVID: Did you.

GRAHAM: You're very funny to meet, David.

DAVID: I'm what ... you mean I don't live up to the ...

GRAHAM: No, no, no, David. You've got it all wrong, an
even if that was the case we'd forgive you, wouldn't w
Ray ... you're very very tired. But you sell yourself so cheap
don't defend yourself. You've got to put yourself out a bi
they'll defend you as much as they can, but when it comes t
crucial issues you're out on your own, David. You haven
done half of it. Well, we'll leave that for a bit and turn to th
more rational side. How would you assess his physic
stature and condition Ray, just in a few words for guidanc

RAY [*closing in on* DAVID, *against the wall*]: Well, about six foc
eleven stone, well covered, fairly good working order
should think.

[GRAHAM *moves up to* DAVID. *Takes off his spectacles.*]

GRAHAM: Said you were very approachable, David. Kick hi
in the stomach, Ray. Get him on the floor. Shove your han
kerchief in his mouth. Kick him in the stomach and the
we'll see what follows ...

[DAVID *falls to the floor.* RAY *throws his coat over his hea*
No, David, let's put it another way for you. It's the simple
thing in the world when you grasp it. You see, take Ray f
example ... this girl Sharon that he's shacked up with;
thinks he's *you*, and when they're in their bed, David,
thinks he's you, and she thinks she's being done by yo
you see. Now it's not quite as simple as you think ... Ki
him again Ray, keep at it ... You see, David, it's got nothi
to do with RESENTING you, nothing at all ... it's j
that it seems stupid that you're not THERE then to defe

yourself, you see. [*Slight pause.*] I think he's ready now, Ray
... have his face done.

[RAY *screws his foot into* DAVID's *face.*]

Mind you, David, you're better than some. For example all
the people in that article, *Sixty Seconds to Live*, they all said
they'd try to be themselves, except you. That was very clever,
David ... much less easy target. You're on the right track.
What's that on the left-hand side of his face, Ray. Is that a
birth mark?

RAY: No, I just did that.

GRAHAM: You see what I mean, David, you were half way
there ...

[DAVID *writhes slowly under the coat.*]

Wasn't I going to tell you a *story*, David. Listen. A man and
his wife went into a pub, and he said to the barman, I'll have
a Guinness, and the barman said with a wink: That'll put
lead in your pencil. I can't write, the man said, saving up *his*
wink for another time. [*Slight pause.*] As a matter of fact, I've
swindled you, David. I usually tell that story at the beginning to ingratiate myself but I thought I'd leave it till the
end with you. Out of PURE selfishness. I like to give my
stories a good airing. This one's off the record, mind you,
but do you know what keeps an old Englishman happy?
Tell him a joke when he's young. [*Slight pause.*] See what he's
got in the bottom drawer, Ray.

[RAY *stands between* DAVID's *outstretched legs and kicks him
in the crutch.*]

GRAHAM: Yes. Don't want him to be typecast.

RAY: He's not moving.

GRAHAM: You know I'm quite surprised at myself, David.
Giving you this publicity. [*Pause.*] Touch you. I wouldn't
touch you with a sanitary towel. [*Pause.*] Where was it, Ray.

RAY: Monmouth Street.

GRAHAM: That was it, Monmouth Street. You had a beautiful
woman with you, David. I remember it so well. Beautiful
buttocks she had. I think it was your wife Ella. She was
slightly pregnant at the time. Nineteen thousand men were
having blood tests. Beautiful buttocks. I watched one,

going like a fiddler's elbow, and then I lost track of it and
watched the other. Backs of her knees ... almost edible
David. I was with a friend of mine from my office. I watched
him come without trimming the candle. But we were walking in your direction, you see, David, and AS we got up to
you ... incidentally when we got up close it was quite
obvious you'd left the top of the glue pot off ... well when
we got up CLOSE this friend of mine RECOGNIZED
you, but he looked AWAY, you see, David, he looked
AWAY. I'M not going to give myself away, you see.
That's what he was thinking. I'M not going to give myself
away. No, but you see, I can ask you NOW, David, what
danger was there of that. You wouldn't have remembered
him even if he had given himself away, would you, David.
What he didn't realize was that the reason he wasn't looking
at you was because you're a dirty leper, you're a hideous
cripple. It is extremely RUDE to stare at hideous cripples
... I don't see any blood, Ray.

[*Pause.*]

GRAHAM [*takes a switchblade out of his coat*]: Let's have a bit of
daylight through his cheek. This. [*Snaps the blade open.* RAY
takes it slowly, and bends down.] Wait. Glamorous, Ray. Too
glamorous.

RAY [*stands up*]: No, no. Graham.

GRAHAM: No? Don't want to leave any false trails. Don't
want to leave it screaming. Let it sweat [*Slight pause.*] How
do you feel?

RAY: I feel quite enthusiastic.

GRAHAM: Go ahead then.

[RAY *bends down, slips the blade under* DAVID's *coat. Feels
for his face. Sound of strangled breath hissing through the gag in
his mouth.*]

Have to make some concessions. Don't want them to think
it was sleeping tablets. All that, Ray. That little number.

RAY: He'll have a new number. [*Stands up, stares into* GRA-
HAM's *face.*] Graham.

GRAHAM: Ray.

RAY [*slowly*] : Graham.

GRAHAM [*slowly*]: Ray, Ray. Ray. Ray ... [RAY *hands back the knife*, GRAHAM *closes it. Replaces it in his coat.*] Well, David, I think that's all, except for a few cheap ironical statements such as Thank you for having spared us the time, and We'll be in touch with you. I expect you're familiar with them ...

RAY [*inaudible*].

GRAHAM: Ray.

Room. Gramophone playing. Lips Flip: Fade up.
Music turned down. RAY *and* GRAHAM *sitting.*

RAY: I met that fellow the other day.

GRAHAM: Who.

RAY: The ... you know ... you KNOW.

GRAHAM: You met him?

RAY: I walked past him. He didn't recognize me.

GRAHAM: He didn't recognize you. He's got a nerve. Not recognizing you, Ray, that takes the bloody biscuit. Was he looking at you?

RAY: He looked at me and then he looked away.

GRAHAM: He recognized you.

RAY: No ... no.

GRAHAM: That was a bit of a moody Ray. Made the game very simple for him so he could understand it, and he blatantly chooses to ignore the rules.

RAY: He might have thought we were jealous.

GRAHAM: All that gone to waste ... huh. No, no I don't ... He's not as stupid as that Ray. It was double bluff. Double bluff. I don't grudge it him, all said and done. He's entitled to do whatever he likes. He's been out of work for six months.

RAY: He's probably on the streets now ...

GRAHAM: Poncing around like a blue-arsed fly and flogging his chops into the bargain. Poor fellow.

RAY: The Salvation Army does a lot for them.

GRAHAM: Ray.

RAY [*picks up a paper. Riffles it*]: Fairlands Mandy.

GRAHAM: You chose that. Silly cow.

RAY: Fairlands Mandy.

    [*Pause.*]

GRAHAM: Give him a ring.

RAY: It's ex-directory.

GRAHAM: Belgravia two one five six seven. Use your Douglas
    Fairbanks voice, Ray.

RAY: Yeah. [*Crouches by the phone on the floor. Dials.*] Hello.
    [*Pause.*] David there? [*Pause.*] Hello is that you David?
    [*Pause.*] Well I'd just like to say we been watching your
    movie ... you know, spell-binding. I expect you've had
    your fill, but I wanted to register it before I leave tomorrow
    [*Pause.*] Not at all. Not at all. You put on a great great show
    That's all. [*Pause.*] Can I know who it is? [*Pause.*] That's the
    game kid. That's the game. You put your finger on it. Just
    wanted to say what a fine showing. That's all ... That's all
    right. Any time. Bye now.

    [*Pause.*]

GRAHAM: Isn't he slow. Oh makes you sick.

RAY: Yes ... ten years time he'll have three face lifts and when
    ever he winks his legs'll jump up in the air ...

GRAHAM: Oh, belt up, will you Ray ... just belt up, go on
    belt up ...

RAY: Sorry.

GRAHAM: That's all right. [*Slight pause.*] What's the selection

RAY: Fairlands Mandy ... hundred to eight ...

GRAHAM: Fat chance. Their selection ... not yours ...

RAY [*turning the page*]: Polish Otto.

GRAHAM: What's it say.

RAY: Polish Otto traps well and is well placed for a wide
    runner. If she can lead out from privately trained Fairland
    she should outstay the field. But she tends to get badly
    baulked if ...

GRAHAM: I'll take that. Otto. Bring it with you. Coming?

RAY: Yes.

GRAHAM: Come on then, Ray. Privately trained, Ray. Huh
    Ray. [*Stands up. Puts on his coat. Fade to blackout.*]

CURTAIN

MORE ABOUT PENGUINS

If you have enjoyed reading this book you may wish to know that *Penguin Book News* appears every month. It is an attractively illustrated magazine containing a complete list of books published by Penguins and still in print, together with details of the month's new books. A specimen copy will be sent free on request.

Penguin Book News is obtainable from most bookshops; but you may prefer to become a regular subscriber at 3s. for twelve issues. Just write to Dept EP, Penguin Books Ltd, Harmondsworth, Middlesex, enclosing a cheque or postal order, and you will be put on the mailing list.

Note: *Penguin Book News* is not available in the U.S.A., Canada or Australia